DAVID SINGMASTER

34
35†
41
46
56
59
60 †
68
80

LOST HOUSES
of Haringey

Contents

The following abbreviations have been used in this book

Locations

B.C.M.   Bruce Castle Museum, Lordship Lane, London, N.17.
B.L.   British Library, Great Russell Street, London, W.C.1.
B.M.   British Museum, Great Russell Street, London, W.C.1.
G.L.   Guildhall Library, City of London, Aldermanbury, London, E.C.2.
G.L.R.O.   Greater London Record Office and History Library,
   40 Northampton Road, London, E.C.1.
H. Lit. &
Sci.   Highgate Literary & Scientific Institution,
   11 South Grove, London, N.6.
P.R.O.   Public Record Office, Chancery Lane, London, W.C.2.

Sources

E.H.H.S.   Edmonton Hundred Historical Society.
H.H.S.   Hornsey Historical Society, The Old Schoolhouse, 136 Tottenham
   Lane, London, N.8.
L.M.A.S.   London & Middlesex Archaeological Society
   c/o Museum of London, 150 London Wall, E.C.2.
O.S.   Ordnance Survey.
M.D.R.   Middlesex Deeds Registers (G.L.R.O.).
V.C.H.   Victoria History of the County of Middlesex, University of London.

List of Illustrations

Cover In the drawing room of the Priory, Tottenham, a watercolour of *c.*1860

Above Lady Bolingbroke, later Lady Diana Beauclerk, from the painting by Reynolds, 1765 (See **The Grove, Muswell Hill).**

Acknowledgements

The authors would like to thank the staff of the libraries and institutions concerned for their help in research. The editor is grateful to Ken Gay of Hornsey Historical Society for his constant encouragement and to Gwynnedd Gosling of Highgate Institution for assistance with the index and elsewhere. Bert Mason of Edmonton Hundred Historical Society and Rev. Joshua Sunshine of the Edmonton and Tottenham Synagogue are thanked for their help with the section on Brook House in particular.

Thanks for permission to reproduce illustrations as numbered are given to the following.

The Trustees of the British Museum, Department of Prints and Drawings, for nos. 3, 20 and 21;

Bruce Castle Museum, for all the Ordnance Survey maps* the cover illustration, and nos. 1, 2, 5, 6, 7, 9, 10, 11, 14, 16, 17, 22, 24, 26, 27 and 28;

Friend's House Library, for no. 12;

Genesis Publications, Guildford, Surrey, for no. 23;

Greater London Record Office, for no. 4;

Guildhall Library, for nos. 15 and 25;

Highgate Literary & Scientific Institution, for nos. 18 and 19;

Hornsey Historical Society, for no. 8;

the Iveagh Bequest, Kenwood (G.L.C.), for the portrait on p.3;

Mr. Louis Klemantaski, for no. 30;

Mr. Sidney Klemantaski, for nos. 29 and 31;

National Portrait Gallery, London, for no. 13;

Note All the O.S. maps are taken from the 25 inches to one mile First Edition, *c.*1864.

THE LOST HOUSES OF HARINGEY

Introduction

The outlying parts of London do not immediately evoke a sense of the past, still less of a past that was totally different. Yet until a century or so ago many of the present streets of terraced houses and blocks of flats were quiet lanes bordered by green fields. Boroughs with some of the characteristics of inner cities like Brent, Haringey and Waltham Forest did not exist and the areas they cover were part of the countryside. Densely populated districts like Willesden, Hornsey and Tottenham were merely villages in a rural landscape which only began to be built up and urbanised with the coming of the railways around 1850. Until the final century of its existence as an administrative unit, Middlesex was a rural county outside its greatest town, London.

Since medieval times Middlesex had a profusion of large houses. They were mainly erected by aristocrats and retired merchants. In the area around Tottenham, comparative ease of access encouraged merchants to build and occupy houses while still pursuing active life in the City, from the sixteenth century onwards or possibly from an even earlier date. These residences, until the Victorian era, were true country houses; i.e. they had land sufficient to supply the necessities of life and much more. One of the earliest known was the Bishop of London's hunting lodge in Hornsey Great Park. The site is now part of Highgate golf course. In Tottenham, the old manor house still survives with part of its surrounding park, and under its seventeenth century name, Bruce Castle, houses the Borough Museum and Local History Service for Haringey. Although Tottenham was extensively cultivated in the Middle Ages, a surviving tract of woodland on the higher western reaches, Tottenham Wood now Alexandra Park, provided sport for royal hunting parties well into the seventeenth century; similarly, the River Lea and its marshes afforded ample scope for sporting fishermen and wildfowlers. With its easy communication with London along the Roman road through Stamford Hill, it was a favourite resort of the gentry. One who bought land and built a house in Tottenham was Sir Abraham Reynardson (d. 1661) whose story is told in this book. Another was Sir Richard Mallory, Lord Mayor of London 1564—65, in whose estate Brook House was left. By the end of the eighteenth century titled people were looking further afield for their rural retreats, but Tottenham was still attractive to businessmen like William Hobson whose home, Markfield House, is also described here. The extensions through Tottenham of the Great Eastern Railway from 1872 with the provision of workmen's tickets on the Enfield to Liverpool Street line greatly changed the character of the district.

Hornsey remained wooded later than Tottenham and was probably largely uncultivated until the twelfth century. Subsequent settlement tended to cluster round access points, notably Crouch End and Muswell Hill on the route to the north, and Highgate on the newer route through the Bishop's park, linked by roads to the City and the inns of Court. From the sixteenth century, Highgate, which was considered to include the area from Muswell Hill to Holloway, drew many people who were prominent in social or political life — Sir Roger Cholmeley (d. 1565), founder of Highgate School, Sir William Cornwallis (d. 1631), Thomas Howard Earl of Arundel (d. 1646) and several Lord Mayors among them. Of the mansions they built, sometimes not even the site is known precisely. But one remains, Cromwell House on Highgate Hill, owing its survival largely to institutional use having been found for it early in the nineteenth century.

Country houses on and around the Northern Heights of London continued to be built throughout the seventeenth and eighteenth centuries. A great-grandson of Charles II selected Muswell Hill for his country residence, and lived in The Grove, as related here. One of the grandest buildings was Harringay House, with its park partly encircled by the New River. Stretches of ornamental water were often to be found on these properties. Campsbourne Lodge to the north of Hornsey High Street had a lake and so did Topsfield Hall, the re-built manor house of Crouch End, and Tottenham Park otherwise the 'Moated House' in White Hart Lane. Gardens and greenhouses were often maintained to the same exacting standards as the stately homes of the shires.

After about 1830 communications with London became even easier. This was due first to improved road surfaces and later to new modes of public transport — horse buses and steam trains. A short smooth ride to town was one of the attractions for a new kind of landed proprietor, the regular commuter. He could settle with his family in the rural environs of London and still go daily to the City. The country home of the gentleman of leisure was now the family home of the successful business or professional man. Before the nineteenth century, the country home had usually been the alternative (for several months at a time) to the house in Town, but after the 1830s the option of living near the place of work was regarded as no longer open. Increasingly the crowded and insanitary conditions of inner cities made it too distasteful. Those whose social credentials from birth or rank enabled them to take part in the London Season could still find the money to maintain a home among the tree-lined squares of the West End, but the luxury of having more than one family residence was becoming unattainable by all but the very rich.

Notable houses continued to be built near London in the first half of the nineteenth century. In the Hornsey area, most of them had a comparatively short life mainly because of the effects of the Great Northern Railway being built across the district on its way from King's Cross to York. The opening of Hornsey station in 1850 and of Wood Green station in 1859, more particularly the construction of the Highgate branch railway through Crouch End and Finsbury Park in the 1860s signalled the end of exclusivity and the beginning of a building boom in middle and working class housing. Just before the railway age, in the 1820s, the enclosures under the 1813 Hornsey Enclosure Act gave additional opportunities for investment since former common land became available for purchase and this in turn stimulated the breaking-up of the larger estates. At the same time rising expectations in terms of space and comfort tended to make new houses bigger as the grounds became smaller. The Priory in Hornsey, for example, replaced a more modest redbrick house; it was a gothic crenellated mansion allegedly built from the materials of Wanstead House when that was demolished. It lasted only until the death of its owner in 1897 and gave way to Edwardian terraced streets. A somewhat similar structure, Southwood Hall in Highgate, survived as a school until the 1930s. Crouch Hall, built for the Booths of the gin firm, was pulled down in the 1880s to make way for the urban development of Crouch End, like Topsfield Hall a few years later. The developer W. J. Collins, who himself lived in Fortismere, was responsible for the disappearance of several other large houses in Muswell Hill in creating new middle class estates, a process that went on in that neighbourhood till the 1930s.

Although the houses have gone, traces remain. Sometimes it is in the names of streets; cases in point are the Priory and two houses in Highgate, Winchester Hall and another Priory, both the homes of wealthy ironfounders, which are all commemorated by existing roads. Often it is the shape of subsequent development, which was affected by particular fields and paths and hedges. To nearly all the houses, local folklore has someting to contribute, though collective memory is fading fast. But quite apart from natural local curiosity about the past, these houses deserve to be recorded for broader historical reasons. Their occupants were not only employers of local labour and customers of local shops and services but patrons of institutions that could depend on their support or approval. The role of these people as arbiters of fashion or of social behaviour invested their most trivial activities with a certain glamour. Often the residence was the background to a life of national, sometimes international, significance. That the houses were in any case an important element in the social and economic history of the environs of London is an understatement; their sheer size and the magnificence of their grounds dominated the rural landscape. Life in the big suburban houses looked secure and enviable. To many it offered a pattern to be emulated, even at the very end of the era.

Historians can view lost houses dispassionately, penetrating the interiors and chronicling the changing fortunes of their owners. They can assemble the evidence to portray a vanished way of life of which certain aspects have become alien to the twentieth century but which must be understood if the past is to be interpreted correctly. Many different sources have been used, some for the first time, and amongst the discoveries are a few previously unknown personalities. The houses in this book are only a small selection of the many that disappeared in the face of rising land values on the outskirts of London. A wealth of documentary material lies in store for future researchers.

The book represents the coming together of two initially separate projects. The first was a series of articles in the Hornsey Historical Society *Bulletin* under the title "The lost houses of Hornsey". It was sparked off by one individual's desire to investigate the places described in 1850 by William Keane in his *Beauties of Middlesex*, although the series soon started to go beyond Keane's survey, to include houses of other periods. It now seems to have been part of a general reawakening, for after it had started, Mark Girouard's *Life in the English Country House* was published, and was an immediate and enormous success. The book broke new ground in that instead of looking at architectural style alone it examined houses as machines for living in and explained how changing social customs and requirements had altered design. Wherever possible, where the evidence was available, this approach had been attempted for individual homes in the Hornsey series. But above all Lost Houses were to be viewed in the context of local history, and therefore not so much as part of a general survey to illustrate a particular social development as places with a story of their own that materially affected the growth of a whole district.

Secondly, a little later, the research for an exhibition at Bruce Castle Museum on rural Haringey produced much material on the big houses whose estates once covered the area. Interest focussed on the links that were revealed between the families concerned and distant countries, now part of the Commonwealth. The desire naturally arose to make this information permanently available for the people of Haringey in particular and for a larger public by incorporating it in a wider publication. So began a fruitful collaboration between the Museum and Hornsey Historical Society. Five of the *Bulletin* articles were revised and expanded in the light of recent findings. The others have been specially written for the book to include some of the new material and thus to extend the coverage to the area of the present borough. We hope that the book will be the first of a series on the lost houses of Haringey.

The authors are all living and working in North London. Alan Aris is an Inner London Education Authority teacher. Sylvia Collicott is a support teacher for the Haringey Multi-cultural Curriculum Support Group. Ian Murray and Jean Pegram are respectively Archivist and Local History Assistant at Bruce Castle Museum. Joan Schwitzer has chaired the Hornsey Historical Society since 1974.

Joan Schwitzer, 1985

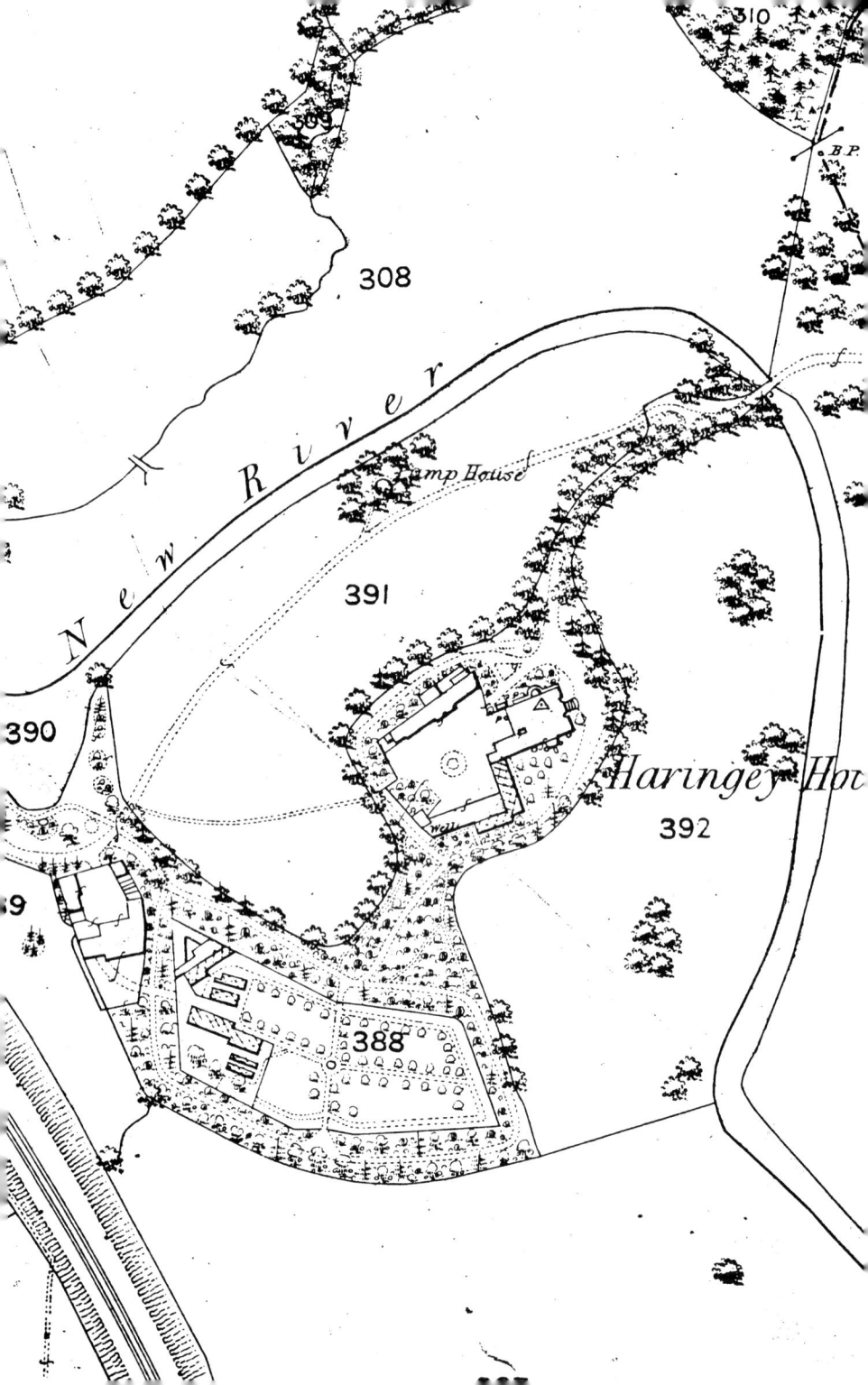

310

309

B.P.

308

New River

Pump House

391

390

9

Haringey Hou

392

388

Harringay House

2

HARRINGAY HOUSE
By Alan Aris

Nowadays it is difficult to believe that where Allison Road in Harringay meets Wightman Road there was once a large house, with outbuildings and gardens, standing in 3 acres of grounds. This house, Harringay House, overlooking a gentle bend in the New River, had commanding views over the surrounding countryside and was the focal point of the Harringay Park estate. When, in the mid 19th century, the estate was at its fullest extent it was bounded by Turnpike Lane in the north, Green Lanes in the east, the Tottenham and Hampstead Junction Railway in the south and the Great Northern Railway in the west. Meandering across the estate from north to south was the New River. Although most of the estate, including the house itself, lay in the old parish of Hornsey a small portion along the eastern boundary was in the parish of Tottenham since the parish boundary traversed the estate from north to south.

Unfortunately, there is no known close-up picture or photograph of the house itself. The best picture available is of a view, from nearby Finsbury Park, looking north towards the house situated at the top of the hill. There are also in existence photographs of various parts of the estate taken before housing development began. A more accurate description of the house itself can be obtained from advertisements placed in the *Hornsey & Finsbury Park Journal* and *The Builder* by the British Land Company when, after their purchase of the Harringay Park estate in the early 1880s, they put the house up for auction on 29th October 1883.[1] The illustration of the house and its immediate surroundings, taken from a plan in 1880, gives an aerial view in outline.[2] Further information about the house and its surroundings comes from recorded accounts by two visitors to the house during the 19th century. From all these sources one may conjecture that Harringay House was a substantial residence and it would appear that the estate was probably one of the largest in Hornsey.[3]

The first visitor to provide any worthwhile description of the property was J. C. Loudon, the landscape gardener, who visited the house on 17th June 1840. From his description it would appear that the gardens of the house were something of a feature at the time:

"To those like us who have known Harringay for the last twenty years, it is interesting on account of the numerous specimens of rare American trees and shrubs which it once contained, and of which there are still some interesting remains. Magnolia macropylla, which had attained the height of 20ft., and flowered frequently, still exists, but was much injured by the winter of 1837—8. M. conspicua and M. c. Soulangeana are 20ft. high, and flower freely every year. There are various other fine specimens, and the place is kept in good order".

He also described the impressive drive to the house, which, he wrote:

"occupies the summit of a knoll, and, half-way down, the New River winds round it on three sides. Agreeably to the old style of laying out places of this kind, the entrance front is on that side of the mansion which contains the finest views, so that a stranger visiter *(sic)* sees everything worth seeing in point of scenery before he alights from his carriage. Something has been done to counteract this, by a fringed line of trees in the fore-ground, close to the gravelled area for turning carriages on, or what may be called the arena of honour, so that the full enjoyment of the fine views is reserved for the walks in the pleasure-ground. This arrangement constitutes the merit of the place as a study for the young landscape-gardener.[4]

However, for what is the best and fullest account on record, our thanks are due to William Keane who visited Harringay House sometime around 1849. He describes his visit in the following terms:

"The house is a handsome and commodious residence seated on the summit of a conical hill and is surrounded on three sides by the New River. The broad open entrance to the gates, with an appropriate lodge at each side produces a first impression favourable to, and in character with, the interior scenes. From the winding and gently-rising approach, a large smooth knole-like hill is seen in the south-west distance; its fine flowing outlines are bare of trees, but on the sloping grounds of the park are groups of different sizes, one is composed of several trees, another of three trees and a third of only two trees, by which a moving panorama is displayed with every step of the beholder. On the other side is a fine oak tree and a large plantation. The road then enters the umbrageous foliage of a large group of trees composed of oak, elm, beech and birch, then over a bridge that spans a moat-like piece of water, through a winding avenue to the east front of the house.

It is a proud situation; the ascent which had been gradual, easy and delightful, is now observed from the fine table-land on the summit, to be a very elevated situation, commanding an extensive prospect over the diversified scenery of the lovely country by which it is encompassed on all sides. The prospects are so varied, and appear in such rapid succession from the facility with which the different points of view are attained, that the mind connects all the beautiful parts or scenes into one wide-spreading landscape, diversified with wood, water and buildings, that give greatness, cheerfulness and adornment to the whole.

The conservatory and greenhouse attached to the mansion are 122 ft long by 18 ft wide and 16 ft high, forming the two sides of a square. No finer or more delightful scene than this could be imagined. In the centre are large camellia trees planted in a compost of loam, peat and sand, that indicate by their large glaucous foliage and prominent flower buds, a robust state of health;... also acacias of sorts, limes, citrons, cytissus, eucalyptus and epacris....The whole is heated by hot water, and forms a delightful promenade at all seasons — in winter it is pleasant to walk through these groves, in the temperature of more sunny climes, or in summer, protected by their foliage from a bright and scorching sun. To the south front, on the pleasure grounds, are evergreen oaks, a tulip tree, and a handsome variegated holly 25 feet high, with a pleasant view of the bright waters of the New River winding through the valley. To the right are the noble magnolia trees that have contributed to the celebrity of this place....

Through the grove, that protects the mansion from the west and surly north winds, are pleasant walks that traverse the grounds and communicate with the kitchen garden. Large evergreen trees and shrubs fringe this plantation, and produce shelter and other effects not to be disregarded in scenes of extent and of grandeur. The kitchen garden, about one acre and half walled in, is seated on a sloping bank and furnished with a peach house and vinery 66 feet long, a vinery pit 40 feet long, and another pit of the same length for strawberries."[5]

Although neither Loudon or Keane mention it, there was another driveway which led westwards from the house into Tottenham Lane close to the Railway Hotel, as can be seen from various maps of the estate. When the Great Northern Railway was built it was necessary for this driveway to pass through a tunnel under the railway. (This tunnel must have been somewhere in the region of where the Schweppes depot stands today.)

The interior of Harringay House is described in the British Land Co. Ltd. advertisements referred to earlier, in the following terms:

"The Freehold Family Mansion known as Harringay House, Green Lanes in the parish of Hornsey, a short distance from Hornsey Station on the Great Northern Railway, and the Harringay Park (Green Lanes) Station on the Midland Railway, containing the following information viz:— Large entrance hall, drawing and dining-rooms, morning room, school room, small drawing-room, library, conservatory room, with room above; large conservatory, waiting room, 12 bedrooms, 2 dressing rooms, day and night nurseries, store-room, billiard room, bathroom etc., the domestic offices comprise kitchen, larder, butler's pantry, housekeepers-room, lamp-room, and servants hall. The outbuildings are extensive, and comprise, on the south side of the yard, laundry, and on the north side, laundry, with ironing-room above, dairy, small dairy, and wash house, stabling with loft, coachman's room, coach house, brew-house, potting sheds, boiler house, greenhouse, etc."[6]

From the foregoing descriptions one may perhaps deduce that Harringay House was an attractive, substantial and desirable residence suitable for a well-to-do Victorian family. Regrettably neither Loudon or Keane tell us anything about the occupants of the house. For this we must turn to other sources to consider the history of the house and estate and its various occupants.

Prior to the end of the 18th century little is known of Harringay House and estate or its various occupants and even the very origins of its name remain obscure. It seems likely that, historically, the Harringay Park estate formed part of the hunting chase of the Bishops of London extending from Highgate to Tottenham.[7] As Green Lanes, running along the eastern boundary of the estate, had long been one of the main roads from London to Cambridge and the north doubtless many historical figures had passed that way. This, however, must remain pure speculation.

The Cozens family were the earliest known occupants of a house which originally stood on the site of where Harringay House was subsequently built. This earlier house, the seat of the Cozens family, was a fine old Tudor mansion which was pulled down in 1750.[8] The last member of the Cozens family to live on the estate, Ida Cozens, sold it in 1789 to Edward Gray, a linen draper of Cornhill.[9] It would appear that it was Mr. Gray who introduced the name Harringay to the house and estate. When he acquired the property in 1789 it was known as Downhill Fields.[10] These consisted of Hill Field, Pond Field, South Field and Collier's Field together with Woodfield and Drayner's Grove. It was about the year 1792 that Mr. Gray erected "a capital messuage or mansion house called Harringay House", with two entrance lodges adjoining Southgate Road (now Green Lanes).[11]

During his lifetime Mr. Gray added to the estate and in 1802 he acquired the Queen's Head Tavern together with 5 acres of meadowland.[12] In 1816, under the Act for enclosing lands in the parish of Hornsey, he was awarded an allotment of waste land.[13] This seems to have been part of Duckett's Common adjacent to the Queen's Head Tavern.

The name Harringay House appears to be recorded for the first time in 1819 and this becomes in the Ordnance Survey maps "Harringhay" (1822) and "Haringey" (1864), while the Survey *Area Book* in the following year calls it "Horingey".[14] However, an 1881 map could still refer to "Herringhay House".[15] Notwithstanding this, Edward Gray, in his will dated 13th September 1833 speaks of his dwelling house called "Harringay House at Hornsey" and his "lands, tenements and hereditaments called Harringay Park".[16]

14

3

4

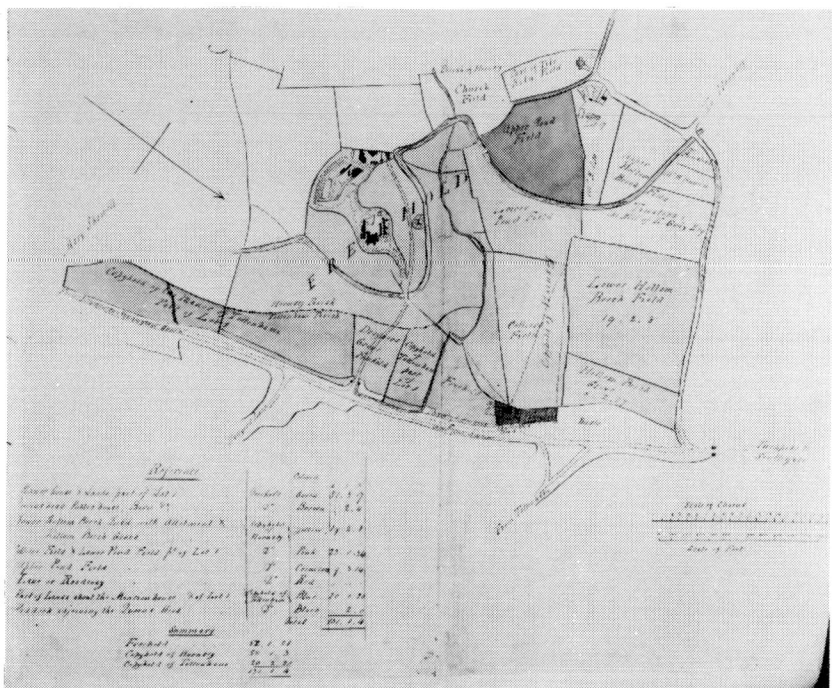

Gray died on 14th September 1838 and his property was sold on 14th June 1839.[17] The new occupier of the house and estate was Edward Henry Chapman but the house and estate were first purchased by William Hobson of "Markfield" in Tottenham.[18] Hobson's role in the purchase and subsequent sale to Chapman is a little obscure but it is certain that he purchased "lots 1, 2, 3, 4, 5, 18 and 32 comprising the capital messuage or mansion house, park, lands, public house and hereditaments.......totalling £17,350."[19] In addition there was a condition to purchase the timber on the estate at an agreed price of £1,473.11s, making a total of £18,823.11s.[20] Another further sum of £43.9.9 was subsequently added for timber making a grand total of £18,867.0.9.[21]

Mr. Hobson, as well as being a building contractor, owned a considerable amount of property and was a property speculator. He may have been speculating in the purchase of Harringay House and estate but he soon shed his interest. In indentures of lease and release dated 24th & 25th January, 1840 the trustees of the Will of Edward Gray jointly with William Hobson did "sell and release to Mr. Edward Henry Chapman, Harringay House with out offices and buildings, two entrance lodges, together with freehold and charterhold".[22] The price paid was £18,877.0.9 made up as follows:

£12,400.0.0 for the freehold land
£4,677.0.9 for the copyhold of Hornsey
£1,800.0.0 for the copyhold of Tottenham.[23]

The map illustration from the Middlesex Land Registry indicates the various areas.[24] It seems from this map that the Trustees still retained a portion of the estate but this was eventually sold to Chapman in March 1840 for the sum of £1,050.[25]

Thanks to improved census recording from 1841 onwards we are able to glean more information about subsequent occupants of Harringay House than had been hitherto possible. Little is known of the Cozens family or of Edward Gray but from the 1841 census we learn that Chapman was born at Whitby in Yorkshire at the beginning of the 19th century and before purchasing Harringay House had lived at nearby Highbury Grange, Islington.[26] In the 1861 census he is described as a magistrate and shipowner.[27] At one time he was a partner in the banking firm of Overend, Gurney & C.,[28] the failure of which, in 1866, caused something of a stir in the contemporary financial world.[29] Whether this hastened Mr. Chapman's death we shall probably never know but he died soon afterwards on 22nd March 1869.[30] Nevertheless, in a comparison of the 1841 and 1861 census enumerators' returns the numbers living at Harringay House had increased during his occupancy. In 1841 he was living there with his wife and two relatives and a staff of 7 servants.[31] By 1861 the number of relatives had increased to eight (though this may have been a temporary house party) and the number of servants to 14. These latter included a butler, a groom and a gardener.[32] Clearly this reflected a prosperous Victorian life-style. Mr. Chapman died without any surviving issue[33] and seems to have been the last owner occupier of Harringay House.

A stained glass memorial window containing the following epitaph was placed in St. Mary's Church, Hornsey:—

"To the Glory of God and in Sacred Memory of
EDWARD CHAPMAN, Esquire
He was born at Whitby, January 16th, 1803 and fell asleep
at his residence, Harringay House, Middlesex,
March 22nd, 1869.
Looking unto Jesus, the author and finisher of our faith."[34]

The executors and trustees of Chapman's will appear to have preferred to let the house and estate rather than immediately dispose of it by sale. Shortly before his death Chapman had sold a small portion of the estate to the Great Northern Railway Company;[35] presumably their operations adjacent to Hornsey station were expanding. However, it was the executors of the will who purchased the copyhold portion of the estate from the Ecclesiastical Commissioners for a sum of £754.2.6[36] It was obtained in March, 1870 and comprised Lower Hollam Beech Field, Hollam Bank Grove, Collier's Field, Lower Pond Field, Upper Hollam Beech and the small portion of waste adjacent to Duckett's Common.[37]

The 1871 census tells us that the tenant of Harringay House was William C. Alexander, a banker, who at that time was aged 30. He was born nearby in Stoke Newington, and lived in the house with his wife, four daughters and one young son. Again the staff was large, with 14 servants including a coachman and two gardeners.[38] Obviously the Alexander family could afford a prosperous life-style. When they first took up residence and what the terms of the tenancy were remain unknown.

It was formerly thought that Alexander had purchased the property after Chapman's death and that he had eventually disposed of it to the British Land Company.[39] From an examination of available records, this was not so. According to the 1881 census records a new tenant, Frederick William Price, was living at the house in succession to Alexander. Also, in an indenture dated 1st December 1880, whereby 24 acres of the estate adjacent to Hornsey Station were sold by Mr. Chapman's executors to the Great Northern Railway Co., Mr. Price is expressly mentioned.[40] There is, incidentally, no record of what happened to Mr. Alexander and his family or when they vacated the house.

5

According to the 1881 census Price, at that time aged 66 and born in nearby Kingsland, was a retired manager. He lived in the house with his wife, son, and three young daughters, the youngest of whom was only four.[41] Also apparently in residence was Mr. Price's widowed sister, aged 73, together with three other relations. The staff had grown in number to 16 and still included a coachman and gardener.[42] Once again the terms of the tenancy remain unknown.

The subsequent sale of the house and estate must have caused someting of an upheaval with so many persons involved. They presumably had to find new accommodation, and the servants new positions elsewhere. What happened to them is not recorded. But by April 1881, the time of the census, the final death knoll for Harringay House and the estate had already been sounded.

The break-up of the estate began on 1st December 1880 when, as already mentioned, the executors of Mr. Chapman's will sold 24 acres in the north-western portion of the estate, adjacent to Hornsey Station and the railway line, to the Great Northern Railway Co.[43] The price paid is not recorded in the Middlesex Deeds Register. On the 23rd of the same month, 75 acres of the remainder of the northern portion of the estate, which by this time was known as the Hornsey Station Estate, was sold to William Hodson of Graham House, Dalston. William Hodson had agreed with the British Land Co. Ltd. in the contract governing this sale to sell to them "the messuage, lands and hereditaments" for the sum of £57,050.[44] The sale included the Queen's Head Tavern, but this was subject to a lease dated 28th December 1865 that had been granted by Edward H. Chapman to George Hanbury and Barclay Field, both of the Queen's Head Tavern, for a term of 21 years from 25th March 1871, at a rental of £50 per annum. The rights of the New River Company were fully protected. There was also a proviso in the sale that the British Land Co. Ltd., would, subject to the sanction of the Local Board and within three years of the purchase, make up certain roads on this portion of the estate.[45]

The role of William Hodson in this sale remains mysterious. According to the 1881 census (where his surname is incorrectly recorded as Hobson) he lived at Graham House, Dalston Lane, Dalston.[46] In the enumerator's return he is described as a contractor, although he is also referred to elsewhere as a brickmaker and builder.[47] He appears to have been a building speculator, since in the Middlesex Land Registers of the period the name of William Hodson appears with great frequency. Presumably he was a man of substance; at the time of the census he was aged 54 and lived with his wife, aged 42, and their 8 sons and 2 daughters.[48]

In another indenture, also of 23rd December 1880, the sale of the house and the remainder of the estate is recorded. The indenture stated that "the capital messuage or mansion house known as Harringay House....also all those several parcels of land adjacent thereto....containing together in the whole 91 acres or thereabouts" were sold to William Hodson.[49] This sale represented the final disposal of the estate by the executors of the will of Edward Chapman. Why, unlike in the case of the sale of the Hornsey Station portion of the estate, the name of the British Land Co. Ltd. was not also mentioned in this indenture remains a mystery. However, the Company did not have to wait long; by an indenture of 5th December 1881 William Hodson sold the house and his portion of the estate to them. The British Land Co. Ltd. now stood possessed of the house and virtually the whole of the former estate.[50] The prices paid in these two latter transactions are not mentioned in the Land Registry records. S. J. Madge in his *Origin of the Name of Hornsey* refers to the indenture of 5th December 1881 and mentions that the price paid by the British Land Co. Ltd. for the house and 91 acres of land was £81,450.[51] As the relevant records of the British Land Co. Ltd., were destroyed during the Blitz in the last war we shall probably never know the price that William Hodson paid for the house and that same piece of land.

The areas of land mentioned in the indentures of 1st December 1880 were 24 acres, and those of 23rd December 1880, 75 acres and 91 acres respectively. The total, 190 acres, shows that an overall increase in the size of the estate during the nineteenth century had taken place. It is difficult to establish the exact size of the estate during the period of its known ownership. In 1837, during Edward Gray's time, the estimated extent of the estate was approximately 176 acres.[52] Incidentally, the half-yearly rate at this time, at 6d in the £1, raised £18.9.6 under the Poor Rate assessment.[53] In 1841 under the ownership of Edward Chapman, the extent of the estate seems to have decreased to 135 acres.[54] By 1844, it had again increased, this time to 155 acres and, with a half-yearly rate of 15d in the £1, was producing for the Poor Rate the sum of £42.3.9.[55] There were probably other fluctuations and it is certain that there were some additions as well as losses during the ownership of Chapman. In a Statutory Declaration of 22nd December 1880, Walter B. Prickett, a surveyor (with an address at 62 Chancery Lane and in Highgate) and a personal friend of Chapman, states that the latter had purchased a small piece of land from the Jenkyn family.[56] How much land and its exact location remains unknown.

The demise of Harringay House and the estate was fast approaching. At first it seemed that the British Land Company intended to preserve Harringay House itself and its three acres of grounds. This is apparent from the advertisement announcing the auction of the house in which it was described as being suitable for occupation by a large family or a charitable institution.[57] However, with building operations beginning in the immediate area, the whole character of the district was beginning to change. It was only a little later that an eye-witness described Harringay Park Estate as being "a wreck in the hands of the builders.[58] Doubtless, therefore, those who might have been interested in purchasing such a house would have preferred to look further afield. In any event a suitable buyer was not forthcoming.

In April 1885 the first advertisement appeared announcing an auction of the first portion of the building materials and fittings of the house.[59] Obviously Harringay House was no more. At intervals of approximately two months there followed three further auctions selling off the remaining building materials and fittings. In September, 1886 even the trees were put up for auction for sale as timber.[60] By the turn of the century Harringay House and estate was only a memory in the minds of those who had been fortunate enough, like J. C. Loudon and William Keane, to enjoy its beauties before they vanished forever.

NOTES

1. *Hornsey & Finsbury Park Journal*, 12.10.1883 *The Builder*, 20.10.1883 & 27.10.83.

2. M.D.R. 1880, Book 41, No. 763; G.L.R.O.

3. William Keane, *The Beauties of Middlesex*, 1850, p.48—51.

4. *Gardener's Magazine*, 1840, p.584. Loudon was the Editor. Quoted in H.H.S. *Bulletin* No. 11, June 1975, p.40.

5. Keane, p.48—52.

6. *Hornsey & Finsbury Park Journal,* 12.10.1883. *The Builder*, 20.10.1883 & 27.10.1883.

7. *Hornsey & Finsbury Park Journal*, 11.9.1886.

8. J. C. Marriott, "The History, Topography & Antiquities of the Borough of Hornsey," p.538, unpublished MS; B.C.M.

NOTES *continued*

9. Abstract of Title of the British Land Co. Ltd., 1882, Acc.178/7; G.L.R.O.

10. M.D.R. 1789, Book 6, No. 91; G.L.R.O.

11. to

13. Acc.178/7; G.L.R.O.

14. Sidney J. Madge, *The Origin of the Name of Hornsey*, 1936, p.19.

15. Accompanying map in *The Suburban Houses of London: a residential guide*, 1881.

16. Madge, *Name of Hornsey,* p.20.

17. to

23. Acc.178/7; G.L.R.O.

24. M.D.R., 1840, Book 4, No. 306; G.L.R.O.

25. Acc.178/7; G.L.R.O.

26.
and

27. 1861 Census of Hornsey; P.R.O. and B.C.M.

28. J. H. Lloyd, *The History, Topography & Antiquities of Highgate*, 1888, p.293.

29. R. C. K. Ensor, *England, 1870—1914*, 1936, p.112.

30. Acc.178/7; G.L.R.O.

31. 1841 Census of Hornsey; P.R.O. and B.C.M.

32. 1861 Census of Hornsey; P.R.O. and B.C.M.

33. Acc.178/7; G.L.R.O.

34. F. T. Cansick, *Epitaphs of Hornsey, Middlesex*, 1875, p20.

35. to

37. Acc.178/7; G.L.R.O.

38. 1871 Census of Hornsey; P.R.O. and B.C.M.

39. Marriott, "History", 539—540; B.C.M.

40. M.D.R., 1880, Book 40, No. 205; G.L.R.O.

41.
and

42. 1881 Census of Hornsey; P.R.O. and B.C.M.

43. M.D.R. 1880, Book 40, No. 205; G.L.R.O.

44. M.D.R. 1881, Book 1, No. 536; G.L.R.O.

45. Acc.178/7; G.L.R.O.

46. 1881 Census of St. John's Parish, Hackney; P.R.O.

47. Lease, 22.9.1863, M1036; Mortgage, 7.12.1863, M1037; Assignments of leases, 11.5.1870, M3294—95; Hackney Public Libraries (Archives Dept.)

48. 1881 Census of St. John's Parish, Hackney; P.R.O.

49. M.D.R. 1880, Book 41, No. 736; G.L.R.O.

50. M.D.R. 1881, Book 40, No. 530; G.L.R.O.

51. Madge, *Origin,* p.20.

52.
and

53. Poor Rate Assessment Book, 23.11.1837, p.21; B.C.M.

54. Poor Rate Assessment Book, 18.11.1841. p.42; B.C.M.

55. Poor Rate Assessment Book, 15.10.1844. p.20; B.C.M.

56. Acc.178/7; G.L.R.O.

57. *Hornsey & Finsbury Park Journal*, 12.10. 1883.

58. *Hornsey & Finsbury Park Journal*, 12.7.1886.

59. *Hornsey & Finsbury Park Journal*, 18.4.1885.

60. *Hornsey & Finsbury Park Journal*, 11.9.1886.

Topsfield Hall

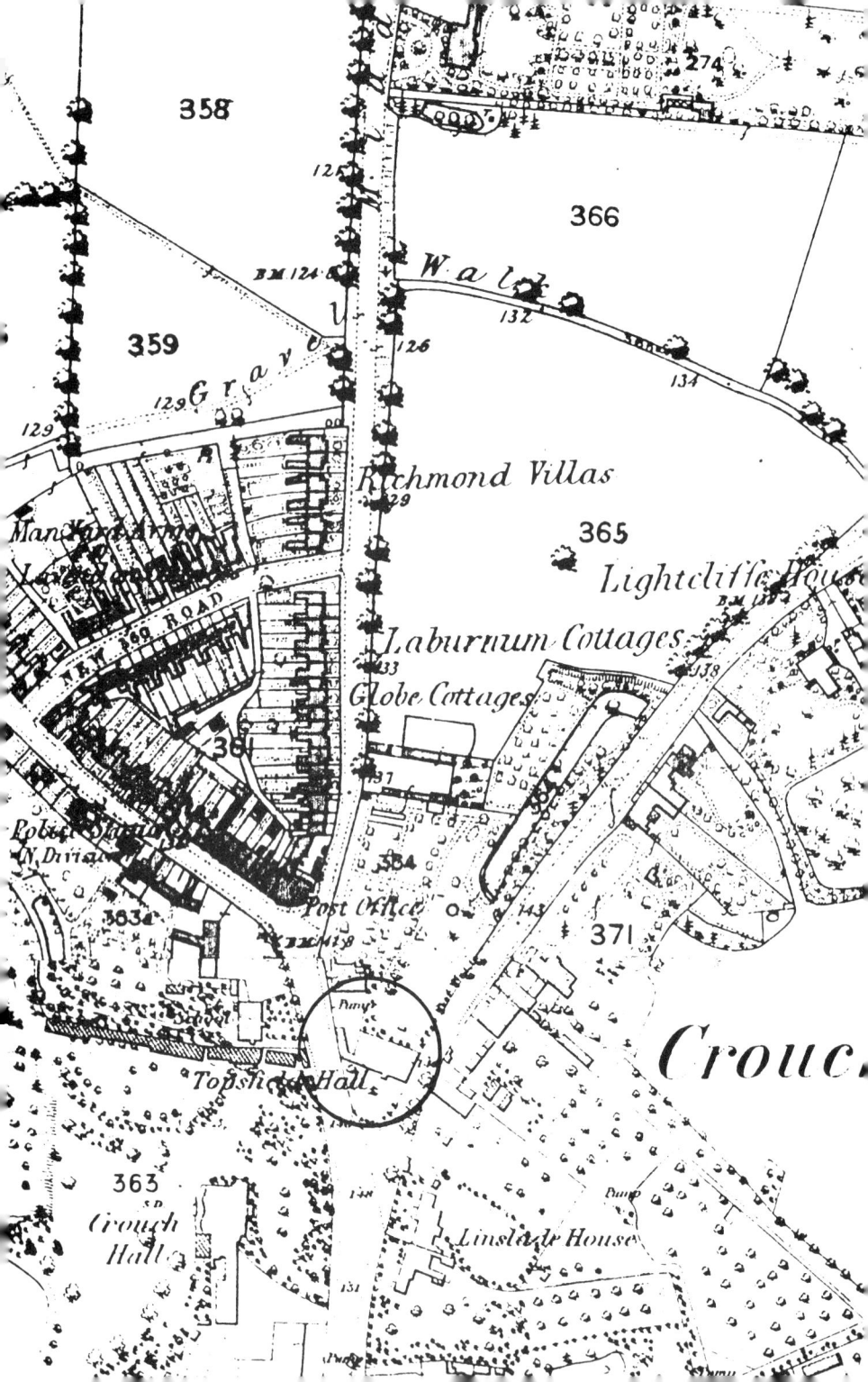

6

358

274

366

125

BM 124

W a l k

132

359

126

134

G r a v e

129

129

129

Richmond Villas

365

Lightcliffe House

BM

Manor

New Road

Laburnum Cottages

138

133

Globe Cottages

137

Police Station

N. Division

384

371

303

Post Office

119

143

Pump

Crouc

Topsfield Hall

363

SD

Crouch Hall

148

Linslade House

Pump

131

TOPSFIELD HALL, CROUCH END
by Joan Schwitzer

Topsfield Hall stood where Topsfield Parade links Middle Lane and Tottenham Lane, by the Crouch End clock tower. It was the seat of the Lords of Topsfield Manor.

The house has been ascribed to the 1780s,[1] but it was probably re-built then from a much earlier house. The coachhouse had been built at least 60 years before since its water cistern bore the date 1720.[2] John Rocque's map of 1745 shows a substantial building on the Hall site.[3] Although the manor courts were often held at a local inn,[4] a manor house certainly existed before the 1780s: "The lady of the manor's stables" are referred to in the record of a court held in 1762.[5] The mere fact of Topsfield Hall being at an ancient crossroads where manorial dues were paid in the Middle Ages[6] indicates an occupation that had begun several centuries before.

Topsfield was a sub-manor, i.e. a separate estate within the larger manor of Hornsey belonging to the Bishop of London, and originated in or before the eleventh century. Crouch End in the Middle Ages was the centre of the cultivated area of the parish of Hornsey, then and for long after an administrative unit. (Hornsey and Tottenham, which included Wood Green until the later nineteenth century, together made up the area of Haringey today.) It was well watered and the tenant farmers built their homes there.[7] The landowner probably did not live on the manor at first, but by the fourteenth century a manor house had been built. A London merchant who paid rent for the land in 1342 is referred to as Richard of Topsfield. Manor courts are recorded from 1374,[8] when Stephen Maynard of Islington was lord. Another Maynard succeeded him.[9] A section of the medieval route to the North that runs from the site of Topsfield Hall to the foot of Muswell Hill was for centuries called Maynard Street. (It is now Park Road, N.8, with a pub still called the Maynard Arms.)

The succession of lords of the manor is well documented through wills and particulars of sales. The estate consisted of 305 acres in 1529 but only fifty acres in 1659, with just four houses on it throughout this long period. By the eighteenth century the estate had shrunk to two inns and rather less than fifty acres. In 1773 much of the land was sold off. Samuel Ellis, the tenant of one of the inns, the Three Tuns where the manor court was sometimes held, was able to buy the remnant.[10] He held a court in the King's Head the following year.[11] Some time after 1781 he had Topsfield Hall re-built. He was evidently a humane as well as a prosperous man, for when he died in 1791 he left £300 in a trust to provide bread for the poor of Hornsey.[12] The house was sold to a Mr. Paul, and the following year, 1792, Thomas Smith of Gray's Inn acquired the lordship from Ellis's executors.[13]

Topsfield Hall in the late eighteenth and nearly nineteenth century can be imagined from the details in the sale catalogue of 1791[14] and on the Hornsey Enclosure Map of 1816.[15] It was a gentleman's residence, modest and unpretentious by later standards, right on the road with no grand sweep of driveway, but recognisably distinct from a farmhouse. The doorway had a pediment, and masks, festoons and wreaths. Behind the oblong brick building faced in stucco, with four rooms on each floor, was a paved yard and a brewhouse. The coachhouse contained a separate harness room and was surmounted by a dovecote. The stables had stalls for four horses. Outbuildings, possibly a cart shed and cowhouse, seem to have adjoined the Hall on the east, along Tottenham Lane. Beyond the formal garden with its lawns and shrubbery was the kitchen garden and the orchard. A length of stream had been deepened to form an ornamental 'canal'. A little way off was the farmyard, where pigs and chickens would have been kept, a barn and lodge for outdoor workers, and the stackyard. There were four fields. All this suggests that despite the small acreage at its command the household was largely self-sufficient, like most country houses then. Milk, butter and cream, ale, fruit and vegetables, eggs, and some meat in the form of pork and bacon, poultry and game, could all be home-produced. Necessities to be bought amounted to not much more than flour, other meats, cloth for furnishings and for clothes, and metalware and tools. Many household articles could be fashioned from local wood.

Smith was succeeded by his son George who lived in Worcestershire and died in 1835. They held the lordship but not the property itself. From 1812 Topsfield Hall belonged, by copyhold tenure, to the Booths, of the gin distilling business, and they let it to a series of tenants. John Gilliatt Booth lived very near, in Crouch Hall, which he had built to replace a farmhouse in about 1833. George Smith's nephew and namesake, formerly a Royal Horse Guards officer, sold the lordship in 1855 to H. W. Elder, who was already in possession of the house. He had bought it from Booth's executors two years before, together with six acres of land to the north and east.[16] So lordship and property were re-united, and for nearly forty years until after Elder's widow died the house was lived in by the same family.

Henry Weston Elder, born in Winchester in about 1805, was a wholesale bristle merchant who also imported sponges. In the 1830s and '40s he had premises at No. 7 Commercial Place, City Road.[17] He married Sarah, a London girl a year younger than himself.[18] His business prospered, and he acquired property in the City and in Kent.[19] He bought Topsfield Hall and its six acres for £3,100,[20] as a country home for his family within easy reach of London. He had one son, Henry Hugh Elder, who became his business partner and heir, and five daughters: Sarah, who became Mrs. Gibbons, Amelia (Mrs. Young), Emily (who seems to have died young), Alice (Mrs. Price), and Clementina,[21] the youngest.

The Elders were "carriage folk", a prosperous couple who could afford to keep their own horses and carriages. They mixed with others of a similar background, as is evident from a Press account of Clementina's wedding. This was to Frank May of Elstree at St. Mary's Church Hornsey on 4th June 1879. She was 29, he nearly 50. Frank later became Chief Cashier at the Bank of England; he died in 1896.[22] The bride, attended by several grown-up bridesmaids — the daughters of relations or local gentry, wore an ivory satin gown trimmed with ostrich feathers. Her father's gift was a carriage and pair. The guests' carriages arriving for the reception at the Hall with a wedding breakfast on the lawn must have created considerable traffic congestion in the narrow roads; a photograph taken on the day shows the staff, with coachmen in top hats, augmented for the occasion by a local policeman.[23]

By Victorian standards the number of domestic servants the Elders kept was not large. This may have been due to the preponderance of females in the family. When the girls were unmarried and living at home, they would have been expected to take on some household responsibilities. The number of resident servants was no more than when the parents were alone and old — two housemaids, a cook, and the coachman and his wife who lived over the coachhouse.[24] But the upkeep of the grounds was a different matter. This would have provided employment for several men living locally.

The layout of the grounds in the early 1860s[25] had changed very little since the end of the Napoleonic Wars. Some of the outbuildings had disappeared so the cows may have gone, but the hay meadows were still there for the horses. Hens were probably still kept, but life at Topsfield Hall was becoming much less rural. Agricultural activities were on the wane, and elaborate horticulture was taking their place. Luxury fruit and flowers were the object. Among installations were a heated conservatory 24 feet by twelve, used as a camellia house and vinery, a narrow

7

8

glasshouse 90 feet long for other vines, a mushroom house and one other greenhouse. The expenditure on labour and heating must have been considerable. Large quantities of tender plants were raised and bedded out in the early summer — geraniums, lilies and dahlias in particular.[26] Several gardeners would have been working while the family received callers and strolled with them by the long pond admiring the water lilies, or played croquet on the immaculate lawn.

What was this impressive residence like inside? A later sale catalogue opens all the doors. On the top floor were four attics shared by the three women servants, so that the fourth one may have been used as a bathroom. They had wash stands, three footbaths and one round 'sponge bath' between them; water would have had to be carried up the 32 steps from downstairs. There was evidently no hot water laid on for the floor below either, since portable bowls also served the principal bedrooms with the addition of hip baths, but the accoutrements were grander — mahogany wash stands to complement the carved mahogany furniture. The bathroom had a six foot 'Roman' bath with a raised seat, sculpted out of one block of marble, and a similar wash basin. As was customary, all the four bedrooms, two with dressing rooms attached, had fireplaces. One contained a four poster bed. On the walls were copies of paintings by Landseer. Carpeted treads with brass rods led down to the ground floor. In the hall were bronze Italian figures of musicians, stuffed birds and a wolf-skin carriage rug. The drawing room contained a large carpet with a floral pattern on a black background and a big mirror in a gilt frame over the fireplace. There were fur rugs, a Broadwood grand piano, a cut glass chandelier, gilt wall lights and rosewood furniture, including a whatnot. Several items suggest colonial connections, with a yak tail brush as a memento of Elder's trade. The contents of the library were

9

unremarkable except for a very old family Bible. In the dining room was a long table, twelve Spanish carved mahogany chairs and an engraving of Landseer's "The death of the stag." The morning room had a more feminine air, with green damask curtains trimmed with lace. The kitchen quarters included a butler's pantry with storage for over a hundred wine glasses. Besides traditional farmhouse equipment, perhaps no longer used, such as a lead-lined salting trough and a pickling tub, there were more modern items, including a knife-cleaning machine and a refrigerator in an oak case.

Mrs. Elder had her own carriage mare and a choice of two conveyances. One was a barouche in a chocolate colour by Adelbert of Long Acre, with upholstery covered in blue morocco leather, and the other was a black phaeton decorated with a fine red line, with its padding inside covered in blue cloth.

Elder died on 10th April 1882,[27] a rich man. He left his wife the possession of Topsfield Hall with an annuity of £2,000 for life derived from income from his properties and investments, a lump sum of £2,000 each to the four daughters and smaller annuities to them and to his sons-in-law. The capital was eventually to revert to his grandchildren.[28] Topsfield Hall was safe as long as Sarah Elder was alive. But in the 1880s urban development was going on all round the estate, and it had become a rural oasis in suburbia. Weston Park and the roads to the north of it were laid out in 1884 and in 1888 plots were for sale. The first part of Elder Avenue, on the east side of Tottenham Lane, was laid out; by 1889 semi-detached houses were being advertised. Weston Park, like Cecile Park, was planned by the architect to the Elder family, J. Farrer.[29]

When Sarah Elder died in 1892, the family decided to sell the whole property. An auction sale of the contents of house and grounds, including farm carts and implements, took place in December 1892. The estate was sold in April 1894. Edmundsons, the builders, bought Topsfield Hall and demolished the house in June. They laid out new roads across the fields, which became Rosebery Gardens and the continuation of Elder Avenue. They put up four-storey terraces of shops curving round to link a widened Tottenham Lane with Middle Lane. At the southern end of the Broadway, the old smithy and cottages, which had been part of the estate, disappeared at the hands of another developer. J. C. Hill.[30] In June 1895, the Crouch End clock tower was unveiled, symbolising the urbanisation of Crouch End. The transformation of Topsfield was complete.

NOTES

1. *V.C.H.,* vol. VI, 1980, p.109
2. *L.M.A.S. Transactions*, vol. VII, pt. 3, W. McB. Marcham, "The village of Crouch End, Hornsey".
3. *An Exact Survey of the City's of London, Westminster, Ye Borough of Southwark and the Country Near Ten Miles Round Begun in 1741 Ended in 1745.*
4. *V.C.H.,* VI, 162

5. Admission by court baron, 2nd January 1762, Joseph Ball, a minor, to inheritance of land 408′ x 25′ "from the corner of the lady of the manor's stables"; B.C.M.
6. *V.C.H.,* VI, 102.
7. *V.C.H.,* VI, 107.
8. *V.C.H.,* VI, 162.
9. *V.C.H.,* VI, 143.
10. *V.C.H.,* VI, 142—3.
11. Court baron, 1774; B.C.M.
12. *V.C.H.,* VI, 200.
13. *V.C.H.,* VI, 143.

NOTES *continued*

14. Marcham, "The village of Crouch End".

15. Original copies of the Hornsey Enclosure map of 1816 are in the City of London Guildhall Library, Greater London Record Office and Bruce Castle Museum.

16. *V.C.H.*, VI, 143.

17. Critchett's *Post Office London Directory* for 1836, p.172. Will of H. W. Elder, 2nd June 1843 (copy); B.C.M.

18. Census of 1871 and 1881; P.R.O. and B.C.M.

19. Will of H. W. Elder, 28th September 1874 (copy); B.C.M.

20. Lawyer's bill to H. W. Elder, 10th April 1855; B.C.M.

21. H. W. Elder's will of 28th September 1874, and will of Sarah Gibbons 17th July 1883 (copy); B.C.M.

22. Potter Collection of North London Topography, vol. 20, p.51; B.C.M.

23. H.H.S. Local Collection; the Old Schoolhouse, 136 Tottenham Lane, London, N.8.

24. Census 1861, 1871, 1881; P.R.O. and B.C.M.

25. *O. S. Middlesex, Parish of Hornsey, 25" — 1 ml.* first ed. 1864; B.C.M. and B.L.

26. *A catalogue of the contents of the residence....for the auction sale at Topsfield Hall, 12th and 13th December 1892, by Messrs. Robinson & Fisher;* B.C.M.

27. Marcham, "The village of Crouch End", p.405.

28. Will of 28th September 1874; B.C.M.

29. *V.C.H.*, VI, 115.

30. *V.C.H.*, VI, 118.

Reynardson's House

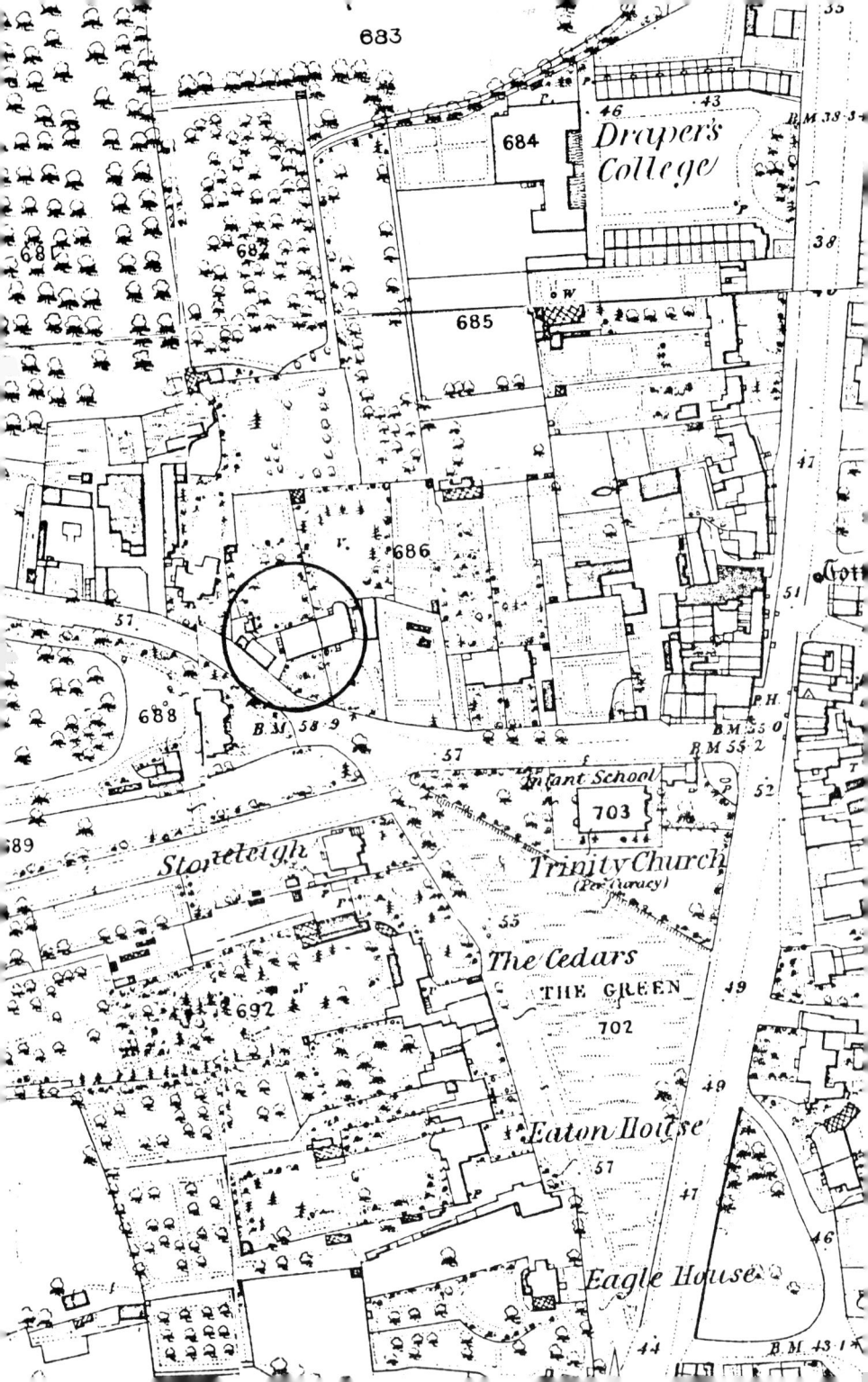

683

684

Draper's College

685

686

57

688

B.M. 58.9

57

689

Stoneleigh

692

Infant School

703

Trinity Church
(Perpetuacy)

55

The Cedars

THE GREEN

702

Eaton House

57

Eagle House

B.M. 43.1

P.H.

B.M. 55.0

B.M. 55.2

52

49

49

47

47

46

44

B.M. 38.3

38

47

51

Cot

REYNARDSON'S HOUSE AT TOTTENHAM GREEN — home of great endeavours
By Sylvia L. Collicott

Tottenham in the seventeenth century was a thriving community, a ribbon development along the busy thoroughfare stretching northwards out of London. The easy communication with the City, for carters and coachmen there were in great numbers, and the relative quiet of the neighbourhood, drew many wealthy London merchants to reside in the district. The Tudor period saw the expansion of trading connections to many parts of the world, the Caribbean, the East Indies and the Levant, and men with such overseas connections came to live in the locality. Sir Abraham Reynardson (1590 — 1661) was such a man.

Abraham Reynardson, born in Plymouth, was early apprenticed to Edmund James, a member of the Merchant Taylors' Company, in the City of London. The Company Records show that Reynardson became a freeman of London in 1618, and was chosen Master of the Company in 1640.[1] His career has been summarised thus: "Sir Abraham's progress in the City can be judged from the following summary of his services. As Alderman he served Bishopsgate Ward from 1640 — 48; Candlewick Ward 1648 — 49 and after the restoration of Charles II; Candlewick and Bassishaw Wards from 1660 — 61. From 1640 to 1641 he served as Sheriff and in 1648 was made Lord Mayor."[2] So the career in the City culminated in the highest office, that of Lord Mayor of London 1648.

Like his father, Thomas Reynardson, Abraham was involved in trade as a Turkey merchant. This meant that he was a member of the Levant Company which had been formed in 1581. The Company was set up because English ships were in great danger of attack when sailing in Mediterranean waters. The answer was to send ships in convoy to secure the Islamic goods so much in demand in Europe. Relations between England and Turkey improved during the reign of James I of England and VI of Scotland, due to the beguiling diplomacy of the first British Ambassador to the Ottoman Court, Sir Thomas Roe. Roe managed to reduce the power of the Barbary pirates operating from the North African coast and secure safe passage for English traders. The increased trade brought rich profits for Reynardson.

Reynardson was also interested in the vast profits to be reaped from trade in the East. He was one of the Governors of the East India Company, newly formed in 1601, and the records show his meticulous concern for the successful running of the Company.[3]

Successful trade enabled Reynardson to buy the mansion on Tottenham Green from a William Younge in 1639. His family came to live there on the eve of Civil War. They were troubled days in Tottenham, with Tottenham families divided in loyalty between King and Parliament. The house was a fine building, as an account, written much later, in 1790, described:

> "It is of brick, large and spacious, in the form of the letter H, having six staircases, two of which are very wide and of easy ascent. The hall, or largest room in the centre of the house, which is now made use of as a school, is square, thirty feet long by twenty feet wide; the floor is of elm, three inches thick. Here are evident remains of ancient grandeur, though at present much defaced; the chimney piece, which reaches to the ceiling, is composed of a mixture of lime and hair to resemble stone, is of a very durable substance, and is adorned with fleur-de-lis and rose alternately in lozenges. Over the mantlepiece in two arched recesses separated by terms, are paintings on plaster; one represents a salutation between two persons, the other a landscape with fishermen, but both are so much defaced as to be scarcely discernible. On

the cornice, whose ornaments have been gilt, are the following letters, A^{R}E 1647, and on the mantelpiece is a shield bearing a coat of arms, which resembles those on the almshouses, except in the colouring which is counter-changed. The drapery and ornaments of this chimney piece are extremely well moulded, and some of the gilding remains. The room was not long since hung with exceeding fine crimson damask with gold fringe. It is called the ball room, for which purpose it was most likely used."[4]

The Civil War was to arrest the fortune of the Reynardson family, as indeed it did for many English families. Reynardson was a Royalist supporter. Why was Reynardson a Royalist? Christopher Hill possibly offers an answer: "The division in England is not Third Estate versus gentry and peerage, but country versus court. Court and government offered economic privilege to some merchants (monopolists, customs farmers, ruling oligarchies in London and other towns) and perquisites to many members of the landed class."[5] The Merchant Taylors' Company, the Levant Company and the East India Company were surely within these privileged groups who therefore supported the King and thereby their own privileged position. Abraham Reynardson was an active officer in all three Companies. While Lord Mayor of London, in 1648, Reynardson was imprisoned for two months in the Tower of London, for refusing to co-operate with the Rump Parliament. During his internment Reynardson may well have wondered if he had chosen to support the wrong side. The return of Charles II restored his faith and family fortune.

Reynardson was obviously a man of considerable wealth and tenacity. Such virtues were necessary in the uncertain political and economic climate of the years of War and Commonwealth. He had cannily raised money from the City Companies for the King but he himself did not pay the Ship money imposed by Charles I. He survived imprisonment and a heavy fine and was knighted by Charles II at the Restoration. Reynardson died in his Tottenham home in 1661.

The Civil War highlighted a great struggle between Commons and King and it highlighted the struggle between merchants and nobles. Christopher Hill so described the events of the seventeenth century:

"The England of 1603 was a second-class power; the Great Britain of 1714 was the greatest world power. Under James and Charles, English colonisation of America was just beginning; under Anne, England held a large empire in America, Asia and Africa and colonial questions were decisive when policy was formulated. The East India Company was formed in 1601; a century later it was the most powerful corporation in the country. At the beginning of our period, men noted as evidence of the topsy-turviness of the times that some merchants were as rich as peers; before the end, many a noble family had salvaged its fortunes by a judicious marriage in the City."[6]

Reynardson's wife survived until 1673 and the house was then inherited by the eldest son, Nicholas. None of Reynardson's descendants were to reach Sir Abraham's poistion, either in business or politics although Nicholas left a local landmark in the Tottenham community, the Reynardson Almshouses. The almshouses were built on the east side of Tottenham High Road in 1737 and were demolished in 1951. The site is now occupied by flats called Reynardsons Court.[7]

The house in Tottenham Green stayed in the hands of the Reynardson family until 1751, when it was sold to Josiah Forster, a Quaker, who established the school mentioned by Dyson. The Forsters probably decided to move to Tottenham because of the strong Quaker presence in the community. The Quakers had bought land adjoining the old Sanchez Almshouses on Tottenham High Road in 1712. Here a meeting house was built.[8] The Tottenham Quakers were to play a vital part in the humanitarian and philanthropic tradition of Great Britain. Members of the

11

12

13

Tottenham Meeting House were among the earliest supporters of the Anti-Slavery movement; William Dillwyn, an American Quaker who lived at Higham Lodge, Walthamstow, attended the Tottenham meetings and was a founder member of the society for the abolition of the slave trade in May 1787. Tottenham Quakers also encouraged education among the Poor (both the Green School and the Lancasterian Schools were founded with Quaker zeal) and offered relief to the needy. Both men and women took part in local good works. The Quakers believed in educating both men and women, thus enabling women to play a full part in the life of the Meeting House and philanthropic works; Priscilla Wakefield, who also lived near Tottenham Green, was such a Quaker woman, writing science books for young people.

Reynardson's house had been used as a school before the arrival of the Forsters. Richard Claridge had held 'a considerable school' for Quakers in the building from 1707 — 1713.[9] So Josiah Forster had a high standard to maintain, for Claridge's school was renowned. Josiah had been a schoolmaster in Coventry and he came to Tottenham with his second wife and a family of eight children. In 1758, the establishment was reported as "a school for boys, where they are taught reading, writing, English Grammar, Latin, French, Greek, merchant's accounts, trigonometry, geography and other useful branches of mathematics, and frequent opportunities are taken to inculcate just sentiments of religion and virtue."[10] It was indeed a liberal curriculum. The pupils were expected to attend the Meeting House regularly. Theodore Compton recalled in *The Friend* of 1885:

> "The chief Friends' school in those days was Josiah Forster's, whose boys sat in front of us little ones in Tottenham Meeting, where, week by week, on First and Fifth days we listened — or would have done — to the Ministry of good old Thomas Shillitoe, Edward Carroll, Luke Howard and Christine Whitting."[11]

Josiah Forster died in the house at Tottenham in 1763, at the age of seventy.

Josiah's son, William, took over the running of the school when he was qualified. When he married Elizabeth Hayward in 1781 he was described as a 'schoolmaster'.[12] But three years later, he gave up the profession to become a land agent and surveyor. He also became steward to the Lord of Tottenham Manor. The school became the responsibility of his brother-in-law, Thomas Coar. Under the new master, the school gained a national reputation. When Coar's wife, Priscilla (sister to William) died in 1799, her sister Deborah stepped in and helped to run the school instead. At some point, the exact date is unrecorded, the school moved to other premises. The school eventually closed in 1826.

Around the turn of the century, Coar had help from the third generation of Forsters in the person of his nephew, Josiah Forster (1782 — 1870). Josiah attended the school established by his grandfather and showed himself to be studious. He began teaching as an assistant to his uncle and then, in 1805, opened his own boarding school at Winchmore Hill, which he eventually moved to Tottenham. He continued this school until 1826.[13]

The Forsters had earned a national reputation among Quakers and a local reputation among the people of Tottenham. Josiah and his brother, William (1784 — 1854) were both active in the Anti-Slavery movement. The Anti-Slavery movement was a mass movement — a third of the membership were women — which campaigned across the country for the end of the slave trade and then subsequently for the emancipation of slaves. The leadership of the movement (the Parliamentary leader was Wilberforce) were in great awe of the West Indian lobby and would take the issue no further than the end of the trade. So although the slave trade was banned in England and English colonies in 1807, and although the

Abolition of Slavery Act in 1833 ended the state of slavery in West Africa, South Africa and the West Indies, slavery still continued. Many countries in Europe as well as the United States of America still had slaves and still took part in the slave trade. William was to die in America, while a member of a deputation to the President to plead for the ending of slavery.

Reynardson's old mansion survived until 1810 when it was pulled down by William Forster senior, to be replaced by two new houses. Ralph Nicholson and Luke Howard lived in the two houses by 1818.[14] Little is known about the Nicholson household but a great deal about Howard's.

Luke Howard, like the vendor, was a Quaker, though he eventually left the Friends for the Plymouth Brethren. He moved into the new house with his wife Mariabella and their six young children. He is said to have been 'a most conscientious and loving father although perhaps somewhat exigent and decidedly austere.'[15] Howard was a chemist by profession but a meteorologist as a hobby. He is known as the father of that science and his achievements are displayed in a glass case at the Science Museum, South Kensington. A wealthy manufacturer, he left Plaistow, the site of the chemical factory (later to move to Stratford) to be nearer his mother who lived in Bruce Grove.

His diary records the day-to-day chores of buying a house and moving in:

8.2.1812	Went to Will. Forster's, Tottenham to breakfast, treated with freehold about his house.
11.2.1812	Walked to Stamford Hill to meet W. Forster about house, returned with him and sister to town.
18.2.1812	To Stamford Hill to meet Sewell and Burnell at 12. Surveyed the premises with them.
25.9.1812	Went with M.H. (Mariabella Howard) to Tottenham about a house of Will. Forsters.
28.9.1812	Went to Tottenham with M.H. to view a house on the Green.
30.9.1812	Met Coar at the house on the green engaged yesterday of W. Forster. Also the carpenter and bricklayer.
3.10.1812	Went to Tottenham with W.H. to inspect fitting up of new house.
7.10.1812	Went to Breammers Tottenham Court Road about chimney pieces (made of marble).
8.10.1812	To Tottenham. Ordered laundry fastenings of J. Pearsons.
15.10.1812	To Tottenham. Met Hopwood and W. Cumber and gave sundry directions about the house.
2.11.1812	Saw W. Forster about Insurance and earth for garden.
8.11.1812	Plan greenhouse at Tottenham to be treated by dung.
3.12.1812	To Tottenham; returned to dinner. Packed and got ready sundry things to go to new house at Tottenham.
7.12.1812	To London with M.H. about paper hangings.
21.12.1812	To Tottenham to meet B. Reid about papering house.
28.12.1812	Chiefly occupied in packing up chemicals for removal to Tottenham.
4.2.1813	Removed with family most part of our goods to Tottenham.
4.3.1813	Evening visited by Will Forster, wife and family.
22.3.1813	Occupied at home on Balance Sheet and planting garden.
30.4.1813	At home (indisposed) occupied in arranging chemical closet[16].

In 1803, Howard gave a scientific paper on the modifications of clouds to the Akesian Society. It was published the following year. Howard indentified and named the cloud formations: cirrus, cumulus, stratus, cirro-cumulus, cirro-stratus, cumulo-stratus and cumulo-cirro-stratus. Howard was the first meteorologist to examine the theory of lunar influence on the weather. Howard studied the weather in the garden of his house. He went nearly every day into London on business or Friends' work, and often travelled to Meeting Houses all across Britain. In his absence Mariabella took the responsibility for recording the weather conditions and reading off the weather instruments in the garden. She wrote to her husband, on the 8th October 1813, when he was visiting Pontefract, "I intend to do my best respecting the rain gauge and thermometer. The barometer I have already attended to. We have had very changeable weather, third day very fine and lightning in the night; yesterday very wet, fine this morning, now very wet."[17]

In 1817 Howard published a book, recording extensively the weather conditions in Tottenham over many years, called *The Climate of London*.[18]

"First M.13. Much wind last night; very fine day: cumulus and cirrostratus. 14. Somewhat cloudy a.m. 15. Overcast with cirrostratus, light breeze. There being no evaporation today, the surface of the snow is a little warmer than the air. 16. Overcast, a slight thaw, from the warmth of the earth, at evening snow and frost again. 17. A clear day."[19]

The work was the result of careful recording by both Luke and Mariabella. The book was to influence two famous men, among many, an English painter and a German poet.

One of them, John Constable, had been given a letter of introduction to London notables by Priscilla Wakefield. (In 1806 he had stayed as a guest of the Hobson family at Markfield House, no doubt also due to the support of the feminist writer.) From the beginning of his career, Constable had been interested in clouds but his early works show no careful study. Stimulated by Howard's book, Constable embarked on a series of cloud studies (these can now be seen in the Henry Cole Wing of the Victoria and Albert Museum). "Having once discovered help for his own art in scientific knowledge, he developed a general interest in the scientific observation of nature."[20]

The other man, so impressed, was Johann von Goethe (1749 — 1832), who was so intrigued that he wrote and asked Howard for his autobiography. At first Howard, in his modesty, did not take the request seriously. Goethe wrote a poem in honour of Luke Howard. The third verse reads in translation:

"But Howard gives us with his clearer mind
The gain of lessons new to all mankind;
That which no hand can reach, no hand can clasp,
He first has gained, first held with mental grasp.
Defin'd the doubtful, fix'd its limit-line,
And named it fitly. Be the honour thine!
As clouds ascend, are folded, scatter, fall,
Let the world think of thee who taught it all."[21]

Howard's fame spread. In 1821 he was made a Fellow of the Royal Society. In 1842 he published *A Cycle of Eighteen Years in the Seasons of Britain from 1824 to 1841*.

In the Quaker tradition, Howard and Mariabella were committed to many causes. Both were in the Anti-Slavery movement. Howard was involved in the Quaker relief organisation for refugees in Germany of the Napoleonic Wars and he was to receive a medal from the King of Prussia for his services. At a time when there was little social conscience about poverty either at home or abroad, the Quakers raised large sums of money to help the distressed. Howard was on the committee to help the Greeks in their War of Independence. The Forster family brought two orphaned Greek boys to Tottenham for an education, although one, Constandine Sotiris, died and was buried in All Hallows' churchyard. Howard was a member of the Society against Capital Punishment and the Society against Cruelty to Animals. He was a committee member of the African Institution and of Lancaster's school in Borough Road. He was an active member of the British and Foreign Bible Society.

The Tottenham Quakers had been among the first campaigners for the end of the slave trade. When the 1807 Act was passed many Quakers turned their attention to the rehabilitation of Africa. In 1807 Howard and his former business partner, William Allen, formed the African Institution. The concern of the Institution was to bring civilisation and legitimate trade to Africa. Their well intentioned interest was to enslave Africans for a further century or more, for civilisation and legitimate trade brought the colonisation of African peoples.

Hannah Kilham, a Quaker teacher, was employed by the African Institution, and she argued for mother tongue teaching in Africa. By 1816 Hannah had decided she must go and teach in Sierra Leone among the freed slaves. She wrote, the following year, "After having finished the little books I am preparing for the children of Sierra Leone, it will be my duty to attempt the reduction of unwritten languages."[22]

After staying in Luke Howard's home, Hannah visited a ship moored in the Thames and persuaded two African sailors to leave the ship and come to Tottenham. There, Sandanee and Mahmadee were educated in English while they taught Hannah the Waloof and Mandingo languages. Hannah then produced grammar books and dictionaries in those two languages. As the young men came not from Sierra Leone but from Gambia, Hannah made plans to work there. Howard corresponded with the Governor of both Gambia and Sierra Leone in support of Hannah's work. On October 25th , 1823, Hannah set sail from London with Sandanee and Mahmadee, now trained as teachers, on board.[23] Howard had provided much of the financial support and considerable moral support too.

The family decided to move to Ackworth in Yorkshire in 1820. Summer visits had been made to the village for some years and the decision was made to settle there permanently. There Howard was to edit the journal, *The Yorkshireman,* from 1833 — 47. Mariabella and Luke were closely involved in the running of the Quaker school at Ackworth. Elizabeth Howard writes of her ancestor, "Luke Howard was very kindly towards the pupils at Ackworth school and disapproved of the severity of the regime there. The children were not well fed. Luke Howard used to invite the pupils to tea for a treat. Howard once complained, 'Friends, I think that if the children had shorter meetings and better food, it would be an advantage to their well-being."[24] She added however, "I am sorry to cast any shadow over this glowing account, but I am rather afraid that Luke was something of a domestic tyrant in his own family."[25]

Howard was to return to Tottenham in 1837 but not to his former home. Instead he took up residence in a smaller house in Bruce Grove. Mariabella died in 1852, at which time Luke went to live with his eldest son, also living in Tottenham. Howard died in 1864.

The two houses built by William Forster on the site of Reynardson's mansion were demolished between 1900 and 1905. Fisk notes in his *History of Tottenham* that a row of shops were on the site. The shops stand there still.

NOTES

1. The Catalogue of pictures at Merchant Taylors' Hall by Frederick M. Fry (1907).
2. H. C. Hawkes, *The Reynardsons and their Almshouses*, E.H.H.S. Occasional Paper No. 41, 1980, Appendix p.1.
3. *Calendar of Court Minutes 1640 — 42*, 1907; India Ofice Library and Records.
4. Oldfield, H. G. and Dyson, R. R., *The History and Antiquities of the Parish of Tottenham High Cross*, London, 1790, p.98.
5. Hill, C. *the Century of Revolution*, 1603 — 1714, Nelson, 1961, p.102.
6. Hill, p.2.
7. Hawkes, *Reynardsons*, p.1—2.
8. R. Collie, *The Quakers of Tottenham*, E.H.H.S. Occasional Paper No. 37, 1978.
9. Biography File on Claridge; Friends House Library, Euston Road, London, N.W.1.
10. Theodore Compton, *Recollections of Tottenham Friends and the Forster Family*, Edward Hicks, Jun., 1893.
11. Theodore Compton, *The Friend*, 1885; Friends House Library.
12. Biography file on William Forster; Friends House Library.
13. Biography file on Josiah Forster; Friends House Library.
14. William Robinson, *The History of Tottenham and Antiquities of the Parish of Tottenham*, 1840 ed., vol. 1. p.106.
15. Bernard Howard, 'A Luke Howard Miscellany', typescript; Friends House Library.
16. Acc 1017/1348; Greater London Record Office.
17. 'A Luke Howard Miscellany'.
18. Luke Howard, *The Climate of London Deduced from Meteorological Observations*, London, 1833.
19. *The Climate of London*, p.226.
20. Kurt Badt, *John Constable's Clouds*, Routledge & Kegan Paul, 1950.
21. Douglas Scott, *Luke Howard, 1772 — 1864*, William Sessions Ltd., York, 1976, p.26—27.
22. Sarah Biller, *Memoir of the late Hannah Kilham,* London, Darton and Harvey, 1837; Friends House Library.
23. Mora Dickson, *The Powerful Bond, Hannah Kilham, 1774 — 1832*, Dennis Dobson, 1980.
24. Elizabeth Howard, *Downstream*, Friends Home Service Committee, 1955, p.22.
25. Howard, *Downstream*, p.23.

Campsbourne Lodge

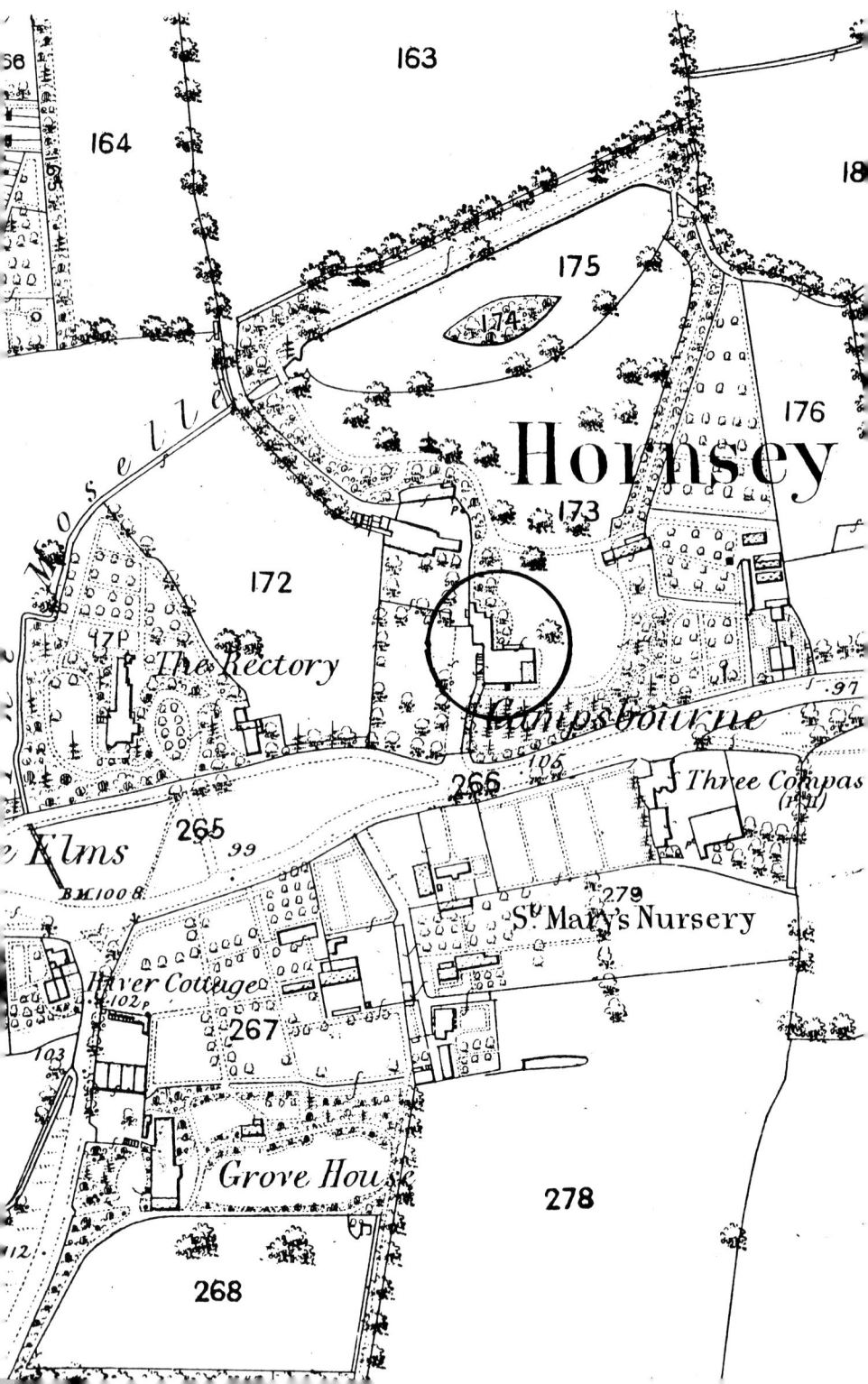

66

163

164

175

174

176

Moselle

173

Hornsey

172

17P

The Rectory

Hornsbourne

97

266

106

265

99

Three Compas
(P.H.)

Elms

BM.100.8

279

St Mary's Nursery

River Cottage

102 P

267

103

Grove House

278

112

268

CAMPSBOURNE, HORNSEY
By Joan Schwitzer

Campsbourne Lodge appears to be unrecorded in prints or photographs, but possibly a watercolour view exists somewhere in a private collection. There was a house on the site, on the north side of Hornsey village, from at least the mid eighteenth century.[1] The same house was probably standing when the Enclosures were made around 1816, and nearly half a century later when the Survey was made for the first large-scale Ordnance map. The property was long established and quite large. The house was classed as a mansion in 1864, one of only two to be designated as such in the whole parish (the other being The Elms nearby).[2] It had ten bedrooms[3] and about 24 acres of land, of which seven were garden and park.[4]

The name dates from the Norman period, "camps" meaning fields, and "bourne" referring to the stream which ran through the property. This stream, the Moselle, was often known by the name of Campsbourne[5] in and around the village. It rose east of Muswell Hill, meandered about Priory Road, and drained into a lake about one acre in extent behind Campsbourne Lodge before flowing towards Tottenham. Enclosure of the low-lying plain used for pasture had probably started in the eleventh or twelfth century. The lake was probably the result of a drainage scheme.

In the reign of James I, the construction of the New River from its source at Amwell to bring fresh water to London, affected the estate directly, and must have led to negotiations with the engineer, Sir Hugh Myddelton, or his representatives. The river was made to run between what became two six-acre meadows behind the lake. It meandered about Hornsey, crossing the High Street three times. In about 1860 the river was culverted underground.

The first recorded owner of Campsbourne lived in Tudor times. He was Sir John Skeffington, a City merchant with other property in the area.[6] A brass of 1520 to the memory of a Skeffington child used to be in the parish Church of St. Mary's Hornsey. At the end of the Napoleonic Wars the owner of Campsbourne was Jacob Warner, who lived at the Priory, nearer Muswell Hill. (This was an older house, not the mansion built on the same site in the 1820s in which Henry Warner was to live.) The Priory estate included 51 acres for the house and home farm, various other lesser properties in Hornsey and the twenty odd acres of Campsbourne.[7] Jacob Warner died in 1832 and his wife, Elizabeth, did not long survive him.[8] They passed on the property to their daughter Caroline and her husband, the Rev. Edward Linzee. In August 1835 they sold it to Benjamin Lawrence who moved in at Michaelmas.[9] He and his wife were a middle-aged couple with a large family and seven servants.[10] In 1843 the place changed hands again, the new owner being William Eady.[11]

Eady was a goldsmith, born in about 1793,[12] a Londoner whose forebears had come from Dorset and set up as jewellers. He married comparatively young for a man of his background, at around 28. His bride was the twenty year old widow of a timber merchant, Elizabeth Hugman, née Cousins, who came from Norwich and already had a son, called William. The couple started married life at the business premises in Red Lion Street, Clerkenwell.[13] Two daughters and two sons were born there. But life in that part of the metropolis had few charms left and the trend was to live outside if one could afford it. So after about six years in Town the family moved to Hornsey, taking a house in the lane known as Church path.[14] Then they moved to Campsbourne.[15]

Eady's firm prospered and by the 1850s 46 men and six apprentices were employed.[16] Eady and his wife were fond of social life and able to live in luxury.[17] Elizabeth bore ten children, of whom the names of all but two are known: Thomas (who went into partnership with his father), George (who became a solicitor), Sarah, Elizabeth, Harriette, Emily, Mariane and Edward. The girls in particular owed a great deal of their upbringing to various members of the domestic staff, rather than to their parents. When the Eadies lived in Church path, there were five servants living in, but at Campsbourne while most of the younger generation were unmarried and living at home there were altogether seven resident employees. As in many other well-to-do suburban households, country folk were preferred. The nanny, Mary Todd from Suffolk, stayed for 20 years; she was still at Campsbourne when the last two of her charges were young women in their twenties. The girls also had a governess, who was said to be very strict. Visiting male teachers taught them painting and part of their holidays was taken up in sketching landscapes. Of the boys' education, little is known; they did not attend Highgate School, though the next generation of Eadies did.

Campsbourne in the 1840s and 1850s must have been a delightful place for young people. Hornsey had remained a village and the other side of the High Street was open space, market gardens and fields except for The Three Compasses, the church and a few old thatched cottages. Campsbourne Lodge, half hidden behind trees, was approached down a short driveway from the road, with steps up to the main door. It had a conservatory at the south-east corner. On the other side was the coach yard with stables for the horses. Beyond, through a gate, was the farmyard and a pump for water. From there a short lane gave access to the meadows, the stream, and, until the 1860s the New River. The water was probably not deep enough for swimming but good for fishing. Across the lawn, quite near, was the lake. It would be surprising if the children had not possessed a boat to row over to the little wooded island in the middle, and if there had not been frequent picnics and outdoor games. On the far side of the lake was a broad walk with big trees behind to shield it from the north and catch the sunshine, trees which also provided shade for cows and horses in the meadow. By the lake was a tall cut-leaved alder with a huge trunk.[18] At each end of the lake was a foot-bridge over the Moselle. On the right-hand side the bridge was linked to a shady path which led back towards the house via the kitchen garden and orchard and greenhouses.

The Eadies were friendly with two other local families — the Birds of Crouch Hall and the Clays of Avenue House, Muswell Hill. They met often and rode round the lanes together. Love affairs blossomed; Thomas Eady married the second Clay girl, Emily, in 1851; Emily's elder sister Elizabeth Jane ("Bessie") married James Bird the following year, and in August 1854 the Eadies' fourth daughter Emily Jane married Charles Clay.

But little more than a decade remained for Campsbourne Lodge. Mrs. Eady was taken ill while on a visit to her relatives in Norwich. Her newly married daughter who was living in Cambridge (where the Clays were the University printers) came over to nurse her, but to no avail. Mrs. Eady died in January 1855, aged fifty-seven. William Eady re-married; his new wife was another Elizabeth, thirty-four years younger than himself.[19] He lived till April 1865. A stained glass window to his memory went up in St. Mary's Church. He probably knew his health was failing for his will was made only a few weeks before he died, on 12th January of the same year.

Apart from Campsbourne, Eady owned other land in Kensington, St. Pancras, Enfield and Bethnal Green, besides his business premises in Clerkenwell. He left it all to a trust to be administered by his executors, who were his son Thomas, his widow and a solicitor. He is unlikely not to have appreciated the potential development value of the estate.

In 1866, shortly after probate was granted, the trustees started selling off the property. Mrs. Eady had moved away to Cornwall. The Campsbourne estate and land on the far side of Tottenham Lane towards Crouch End[20] were sold to the British Freehold Land Company.[21] About a year later , on 16th September 1867, the company held a public auction in the City at the Guildhall Hotel, Gresham Street. Parcelling the land into potential building plots was thought to raise the value. But so much was on offer elsewhere at the time that not all was sold. The eastern side and the meadows were bought by W. E. Whittingham, and Campsbourne Road was laid out. The rest awaited a buyer till February 1868, when John Jay (who lived a stone's throw away in "Ashford", a detached house in Priory Road) bought the house, out-buildings and remaining land for £3,250.[22] Campsbourne Lodge was pulled down and the grounds disappeared under a grid of small streets, bearing names associated with a vanished era — Myddelton, Brook, Moselle and Campsbourne.

NOTES

1. John Rocque's *Topographical map of the county of Middlesex*, 1754.
2. *Area Book* to accompany Hornsey Parish Plan, O.S. Middlesex 1864; Map Library, B.L.
3. *V.C.H.*, VI, 109
4. *Area Book*, 1864.
5. *V.C.H.* VI, 102.
6. Edwin Monk, *Memories of Hornsey*, (first pub. 1976) revised ed. 1978, p.36.
7. Hornsey Rate Book, DRO 20/E2/3; G.L.R.O.
8. F. T. Cansick, *Epitaphs....of Hornsey* (1875), p.13.
9. Indenture between Edward and Caroline Linzee and Benjamin Lawrence in British Land Co. Schedule of deeds (29.2.1868), Acc. 869/267; Hornsey Rate Book, DRO 20/E2/9 and 10; G.L.R.O.
10. Enumerators' Returns, Census of Hornsey 1841; P.R.O. and B.C.M.
11. Indenture between Lawrence and Eady etc., 25.8.1843, in Schedule as in note 8.

12. Census of Hornsey, 1851 and 1861; P.R.O. and B.C.M.
13. Pigot's *Commercial Directory of London 1832—4*. Critchett's *Post Office Directory of London*, 1836, p.166.
14. Hornsey Rate Books, DRO 20/E2/9 (G.L.R.O.) and D/PH/3C/8 and 9 (B.C.M.) and Census of Hornsey 1841.
15. Kelly's *P.O. Middlesex Directory*, 1845.
16. Census 1851.
17. Personal information about the Eady family is based on the unpublished "Records of the Clay family" (1908) by Mary Aimée Clay, grand-daughter of William and Elizabeth Eady, in the archives of the H.Lit. & Sci.
18. William Keane, *The Beauties of Middlesex*, 1850, p.254—5.
19. Census of Hornsey 1861.
20. M.D.R. 1866, Book 17, No. 926; G.L.R.O.
21. *V.C.H.*, VI, 113.
22. M.D.R. 1866, Book 25, No. 236; G.L.R.O.

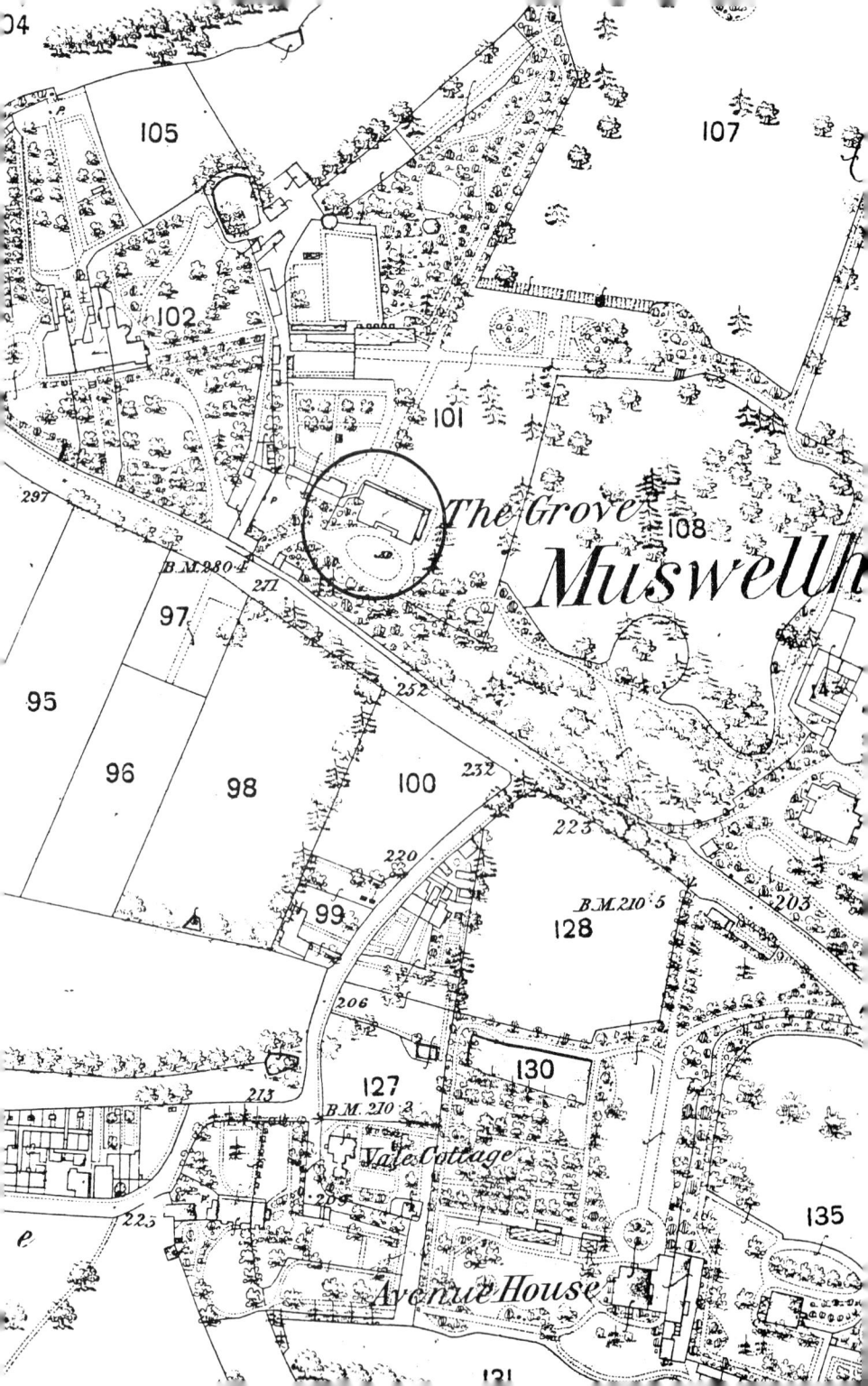

105

107

102

101

The Grove

108

Muswellh

297

BM.280·4

271

97

252

95

96

98

100

232

223

220

99

B.M.210·5

203

128

206

130

127

BM.210·2

e

225

Vale Cottage

135

Avenue House

131

The Grove

THE GROVE, MUSWELL HILL
By Joan Schwitzer

This house was well known during its century of existence, but it seems not to have been depicted in old prints, or none have survived. Its best known memorial of this kind is the view down Muswell Hill in 1822 by Baynes, with the lodge and entrance gates to The Grove on the left of the picture, but the house itself hidden behind trees. A small pen and wash drawing[1] of about 1800 is apparently the only complete illustration. It shows a three-storey house with nine windows across the upper floors and a central portico with ionic columns; pedimented projections are at each end. A carriage drive flanks the lawn in front. The Grove would seem from the style to have been built in the second half of the eighteenth century. Rocque's map of 1754[2] shows the site to have been surrounded by fields with buildings in roughly the same position as The Grove and its out-buildings, so probably an earlier farmhouse was replaced by the new mansion.

The Grove seems to have taken its name from the location. "Muswell Hill grove", varying from a quarter to half an acre of woodland, is mentioned several times in the Hornsey Manor court rolls between 1652 and 1696. It had belonged in the earlier part of that period to Richard Sprignell of Cromwell House, Highgate.[3] In the Middle Ages, Muswell Hill was almost certainly wooded on both sides. By Georgian times the north-eastern side and the crown of the hill had long been enclosed and cultivated and the Common lay to the west. But the garden of The Grove contained a large number of trees, particularly bordering the road and along the boundary with Grove Lodge. Bath House, a little higher up the hill, was similarly secluded.[4]

The Grove has been known primarily as the summer residence of Topham Beauclerk, born in 1739, the great-grandson of Charles II and Nell Gwynn. His portrait shows a young man with a long nose, full mouth and slightly insolent gaze.[5] He was undoubtedly handsome and lively, but had a fatal weakness for pleasure-seeking. While he was at Oxford, he and a fellow-undergraduate, Bennet Langton, became life-long friends of the writer and lexicographer, Dr. Johnson, who called them 'Lanky' and 'Beau'. No one else, declared Johnson's biographer Boswell, dared to take such liberties with the great man as Beau.[6]

Beau married 'Lady Di', an older woman, the mother of three children, who welcomed his advances during her unhappy first marriage to Lord Bolingbroke.

Her divorce was achieved by Act of Parliament in 1768 and two days later her wedding to Beau took place. Diana Spencer (1734 — 1808), daughter of the second Duke of Marlborough, was an accomplished painter whose work was much admired. Her portrait by Sir Joshua Reynolds hangs in Kenwood House. She and her new husband set up an intellectual and artistic ménage and entertained frequently.

The Grove was only one of twelve houses that the Beauclerks lived in during their short married life, but they had it as an easily accessible country retreat for ten out of the twelve years. It followed one at Cookham-on-Thames. Muswell Hill was chosen for its elevated situation and beautiful views. This was sometime before November 1769 when the lease was signed. A contemporary drawing gives an idea of the features that appealed: bewigged people strolling up to the Green Man, farm work going on near the pound on the brow of the hill, and miles of open country beyond.[7]

The landscaping of the grounds of the Grove was commissioned, and about two acres were surrounded with brick walls to form a sheltered garden. Pondfield, one of the original four small meadows, was the site chosen for the kitchen garden and the cow byre.[8] In the house Beau set up an observatory, with a resident astronomer, and a laboratory for his chemical experiments. For the playboy was also a Fellow of the Royal Society and made scientific investigations.[9] At his town house he amassed a library of about 30,000 volumes, covering most branches of learning, including scientific works as well as classical and contemporary literature, and numerous surveys of counties.[10] He is said to have been in the habit of sending a servant very early in the morning to premises where book auctions were to take place later in the day with instructions to buy the cream of the collections, and inspecting the haul on his return from a night's carousal and gaming.

Dr. Johnson was the Beauclerks' guest more than once and left his name associated with the celebrated avenue of elms in the grounds. John Wilkes, the radical M.P. for Middlesex, dined at the Grove, and also Horace Walpole (1717 — 1797), who possessed some of Lady Diana's drawings.[11]On one occasion Walpole was there with Sir Joseph Banks (1743 — 1820) and Daniel Solander, the botanists who had accompanied Captain Cook round the world. This may have been a rather awkward occasion since Walpole believed the voyage had been the spearhead of European intrusion in the Pacific.[12] On the other hand, he and Banks, like others among the Beauclerks' circle, had something in common: they both strongly opposed slavery and the international slave trade.[13] Banks and Johnson employed black men as personal servants: William Sancho, the son of the black writer Ignatius Sancho, was Banks's library assistant; Johnson (who was a friend of Ignatius Sancho) employed Francis Barber, whose education as a grammar school boarder from the age of seven he had paid for.[14] It is possible that the Beauclerks too were involved with the national campaign against the slave trade and against slavery in the colonies and elsewhere.

The splendours of the Grove and its social gatherings became so renowned that uninvited callers proliferated. The Beauclerks felt driven to issue tickets giving permission to view.[15] As a summer retreat it was too accessible. Meanwhile the pace and scope of Beau's activities, particularly the late hours and drug-taking, were ruining his health. In December 1779 Beau transferred his unexpired lease (which had 45½ years to run) on the Grove and let his town house as well to someone called Thomas Walker.[16] (The town house still exists, on the north side of Great Russell Street between Gower Street and Tottenham Court Road.) Beau died the following year at the age of forty-one. Lady Diana made a home in Twickenham and sold the famous library. She brought up her children and did some of her best paintings and murals. She and Lord Charles Spencer were the executors of her husband's will and in May 1782 they sold the lease, which Walker, who lived in Oxfordshire, was relinquishing.

The purchaser of the estate was John Porker, a City banker.[17] Muswell Hill was still a place for the rich. In 1792 *The Ambulator* declared:

"There is not within one hundred miles of London a village more rural and pleasant, or that can boast of prospects so various and extensive. Baron Kutzleben has a pleasant villa at the bottom of the hill. Mr. Porker, the banker, enjoys an enchanting retreat near the top, together with 15 acres of garden and pleasure grounds, laid out in the finest taste by the late Mr. Topham Beauclerk.[18]"

The Porkers were in possession of the property for more than thirty years. John Porker died in December 1808 aged 76, his wife Sarah, eleven years younger, following him within a fortnight, to be buried in the same grave at Friern Barnet church. Their son, also called John, stayed on, but perhaps after the Hornsey Enclosure Act of 1813 he foresaw a new wave of building and the end of rural exclusiveness. He remained till 1816 but by October 1818, when he sold his newly acquired piece of the Common in front of the estate, he had moved out. He died at Tunbridge Wells in 1834.[19] The new occupant of the Grove was William Johnstone, who had a business address in Berners Street.[20]

Johnstone was a prosperous stockbroker, born in 1753,[21] who before settling in Muswell Hill had lived in the parish of All Hallows' Tottenham and in Stoke Newington. He and his wife Sarah had three sons, William, Edmund and Charles. We know almost nothing of their life at the Grove except that towards the end of their two decades of residence a shadow was beginning to fall across it. Charles, born in 1804, who married in his early twenties and had four children, launched into ambitious and expensive financial ventures. He became chairman of a chartered banking company with branches in Australia and of a gold-min ing company in South America, but these joint stock companies did not prosper and the shareholders became very dissatisfied. To help his son, Charles's father was prepared to write off half a làrge loan he had given him. A sad-looking, bald-headed man, he died in 1836, long before the worst trouble came — Charles's mental breakdown resulting in permanent incarceration in an asylum. William and Edmund must have been affected by their brother's experience. Neither married. William followed his father's profession and died in early middle age. Edmund shared his home at Winchmore Hill with his widowed mother, who died in 1851.[22]

From 1837 William Block was the owner-occupier of the Grove.[23] He was a silk merchant, born in 1793. He and his wife Elizabeth[24] who came from Worcestershire, became part of the social network of Anglican gentry. Among their friends were Anthony Salvin the architect and his family, who lived at East Finchley.[25] A brother, Allan Williams Block, and his wife Parthenia lived in Highgate, at "Parkfield"[26] (the predecessor of "Witanhurst"), and were active in local church work.[27] The Blocks lived in style, with five house servants (four women and one man), usually country-born. The coachman and his family lived in the entrance lodge.[28] Block retired from business life early, perhaps in order to have time to enjoy his domain. In 1847 he acquired the old Bath House mansion next door which had been divided into three separate houses, paying £3,800 for it. He also bought meadow land on the opposite side of Muswell Hill, no doubt to prevent immediate development but also as a long-term investment.[29] Altogether the estate now consisted of about 24 acres.

Part of it was recorded in about 1860 by George Shadbolt,[30] a pioneer photographer who lived locally. One of his views and the large -scale Ordnance map of the same period[31] show that a verandah ran along the east side of the house and was continued along the entire garden front. Depite being able to sit there in the shade on a summer's day, a gentleman in formal clothes, presumably Mr. Block, sits in the photograph uncomfortably posed on an upright chair on the lawn. In front of him, the slope rises gently to one end of the famous avenue. To the right, recorded in two other views, is an elaborate formal garden with a stone balustrade separating it from the main lawn. From deeds and plans we know that on the hill to the left was the walled kitchen garden, two big glasshouses and the orchard, also a yard with pig styes and shelter for cows and chickens, a cart lodge and stabling for the carriage horses.[32] The fullest account of the estate is in Keane's *Beauties of Middlesex*. Both greenhouses were heated and one, about 75 feet long, contained rare exotic plants; the other was divided into three vineries. A small park containing fine shrubs and

16
17

trees lay to the east of the avenue, and presumably dated from the Beauclerks' time. The size of the specimens was remarkable; for instance, two rhodedendrons each measured thirty-three feet in circumference. Spanish chestnuts had trunks over twelve feet round, and the biggest, possibly the biggest in England a later writer maintained, was over 18 feet round.[33] There were very large Turkey and English oaks, a 'true Cornish elm', a fern-leaved beech, and a deciduous cypress. Paths through the shrubbery and along the other side of the park led to the farthest point of the pleasure grounds, overlooking the meadows. The view was spectacular. On a good day it was possible to see the sails of ships in the Thames and beyond them Epping Forest and the hills of Hertfordshire.[34]

Muswell Hill was still a village, and rather isolated, with little public transport available for going further afield. An omnibus took people into Town, and the Finchley coach passed through once a day on weekdays only.[35] As early as 1844 the possibility of a local railway was being discussed and there appeared to be a threat to the Grove. Not everyone was hostile to the idea; one view was that a railway would open up scenery which was the preserve of a lucky few to the enjoyment of the multitude.[36] Hornsey Station on the Great Northern opened in 1850, but for the time being Muswell Hill was left alone. In 1858, however, a pamphlet was published advocating a similar building to the Crystal Palace for the northern heights of London at Muswell Hill and proposing a railway from Finsbury Park terminating under the building itself.[37]

Block did not live to see the demolition of his house when the branch line was constructed from Highgate through Muswell Hill to Alexandra Palace for the opening in 1873. He died on 31st October 1861. His three executors — his brother, nephew and a friend, arranged to sell the estate by auction the following June. Of the seven lots on offer, Bath House and land nearest to Crouch End went,[38] but the rest remained unsold. It was just before the railway boom and the nearest line out of London, the Highgate to Edgware, had not yet reached the drawing-board. While the horse and carriage, or Shanks's pony, remained the best aids to mobility and while there was no immediate prospect of large-scale local employment, there was little to attract the speculative builder to Muswell Hill. In a year, however, the situation changed entirely. 1863 was a fertile year of new public enterprises, and some of these affected the district directly. On 5th June, the Grove and designated building plots facing the entrance, on the opposite side of Muswell Hill, were bought by John Thomas Emmet of Islington for £10,650.[39] The Grove was then sold to the Alexandra Park Company, who had already bought Tottenham Wood Farm to form a public park in which a people's palace was eventually to be erected. Access from the main road had now been provided. The park was opened almost at once, in the summer of 1863. The grounds of the Grove, especially 'Dr. Johnson's walk' (the avenue of elms), were to be an important component of the park. The house itself remained standing for only a few more years,[40] until the construction of the railway.

The convenient proximity of the Grove area of Alexandra Park to the Green Man was celebrated in a history of the locality in verse published in about 1880:[41]

> "...see the wooded grove,
> That verdant spot all unadorned by art,
> Where stately trees and grateful shade impart;
> Whose gnarled and mossy trunks bespeak their age
> And stern resistance to the winter's rage...

> Enough of reminiscences like these.
> Come London's toilers wander where you please
> See all the sights, enjoy the lovely views,
> Or, on the shining water take a cruise;
> While, if it suits your pleasure, better still,
> Bring your own "grub" and picnic on the Hill,
> Or in the Grove; yet bear in mind that here
> There is no lack of means to make good cheer,
> From champagne to a penny glass of beer,
> Besides a good cold dinner for a shilling,
> As long as the proprietor's name is *Willing*..."

The last line quoted was a pun on the name of the landlord of the pub.

The Green Man still stands but has been re-built. The branch railway from Finsbury Park to Alexandra Palace closed in the 1950s. In 1980 the second Palace was destroyed by fire. But the Grove has kept its identity and remains a favourite local amenity.

NOTES

1. Original in B.C.M. Reproduced in *V.C.H.,* VI, facing p.33.
2. *A Topographical Map of the County of Middlesex*, reprinted by L.M.A.S, 1971.
3. W. McB. and F. Marcham (eds.), *Court rolls of the Bishop of London's Manor of Hornsey 1603 — 1701*, 1929, p.117, 143, 210, 233.
4. Hornsey Enclosure Map, 1816; copies in B.C.M. and G.L.
5. By F. Cotes. Reproduced in Mrs. Stewart Erskine's *Lady Diana Beauclerk, her life and work,* 1903, on which most of the personal details regarding the Beauclerks given here is based.
6. Robert Lynd, *Dr. Johnson and company,* Penguin 1946, p.72.
7. Pen and wash drawing by Chatelain, "On Muswell Hill" in interleaved copy of Lysons's *Environs of London;* G.L.
8. M.D.R. 1782, Book 2, No. 242, listing appurtenances; G.L.R.O.
9. F.W.M. Draper, "Topham Beauclerk at the Grove", *Hornsey Journal* 17th June 1960.
10. *Bibliotheca Beauclerkiana. A Catalogue of the Large and Valuable Library of the late Hon. Topham Beauclerk... Auction at the Society for the Encouragement of Arts and Manufactures, 9th April 1781 and 49 following days;* B.L.
11. Germaine Greer, *The obstacle race,* 1979, p.290.
12. Walpole to Rev. Mr. Cole, 15th June 1780, *Letter of Horace Walpole,* ed. by C. B. Lucas (Newnes 1904), p.651.
13. Nigel File and Chris Power, *Black settlers in Britain 1555 — 1958,* 1981, p.2.

NOTES *continued*

14. Folarin Shyllon, *Black people in Britain 1555 — 1833,* 1977, p.23, 31. For Francis Barber, see *Notes & Queries,* March 1984, p.8—9.
15. F. W. M. Draper, *Muswell Hill past and present,* 1936, p.11.
16. M.D.R. 1779, Book 5, Nos. 494 and 495; G.L.R.O.
17. M.D.R. 1782, Book 2, No. 242; G.L.R.O.
18. *The Ambulator, or, a pocket companion in a tour round London within the circuit of 25 miles...,* 1st ed., p.164.
19. Frederick Teague Cansick, *A Collection of Curious and Interesting Epitaphs, copied from the existing monuments of Distinguished and Noted Characters in the Churches and Churchyards of Hornsey, Tottenham, Edmonton, Enfield, Friern Barnet and Hadley, Middlesex,* 1875, p.109
20. Hornsey rate book 1812 — 1816, DRO 20/E2/1; M.D.R. 1818, Book 7, 526; G.L.R.O. Pigot's *Directory of Middlesex* 1826 — 7.
21. Potter Collection of North London Topography, vol. 20, p.70; B.M. Dept. of Prints and Drawings.
22. Johnstone family papers; Acc. 1293, G.L.R.O.
23. Hornsey rate book; DRO 20/E2/10, G.L.R.O.
24. Census of Hornsey, Enumerators' Returns, 1841, 1851, 1861; P.R.O. and B.C.M.
25. Diary of Eliza Anne Salvin; unpublished MS. in L.B. of Barnet Local Collection.
26. Kelly's *Directory of Middlesex* 1845, 1858.
27. Samuel Wiswould, *Charitable foundations of St. Pancras,* 1863, p.31. Managers' Minutes, Archives of St. Michaels C. of E. School (Highgate).
28. Census of Hornsey, 1851 and 1861; P.R.O. and B.C.M.
29. The transaction is recorded in M.D.R. 1862, Book 16, No. 683; G.L.R.O.
30. Shadbolt Collection; B.C.M.
31. *Middlesex, Parish of Hornsey, O.S. 25" — 1 ml.,* 1864 (1st ed.), sheet XII, 5; B.L. and B.C.M.
32. M.D.R. 1863, Book 11, No. 888; G.L.R.O.
33. J. H. Lloyd, *History of Highgate,* 1888, p.290
34. William Keane, *The Beauties of Middlesex,* 1850, p.239 — 241.
35. Draper, *Muswell Hill past and present,* p.17.
36. Lloyd, p.289.
37. "Alexandra Palace", printed discussion document, produced by L.B. of Haringey Working Party, 1979, p.7.
38. M.D.R. 1862, Book 16, No. 683; G.L.R.O.
39. M.D.R. 1863, Book 11, No. 888; G.L.R.O.
40. James Thorne, *The Environs of London,* 1876, p.443.
41. W. H. Dance, *Muswell Hill, or, The Northern Heights of London (n.d.). Printed by E. W. Berrill, Barnet; B.L.*

Winchester Hall

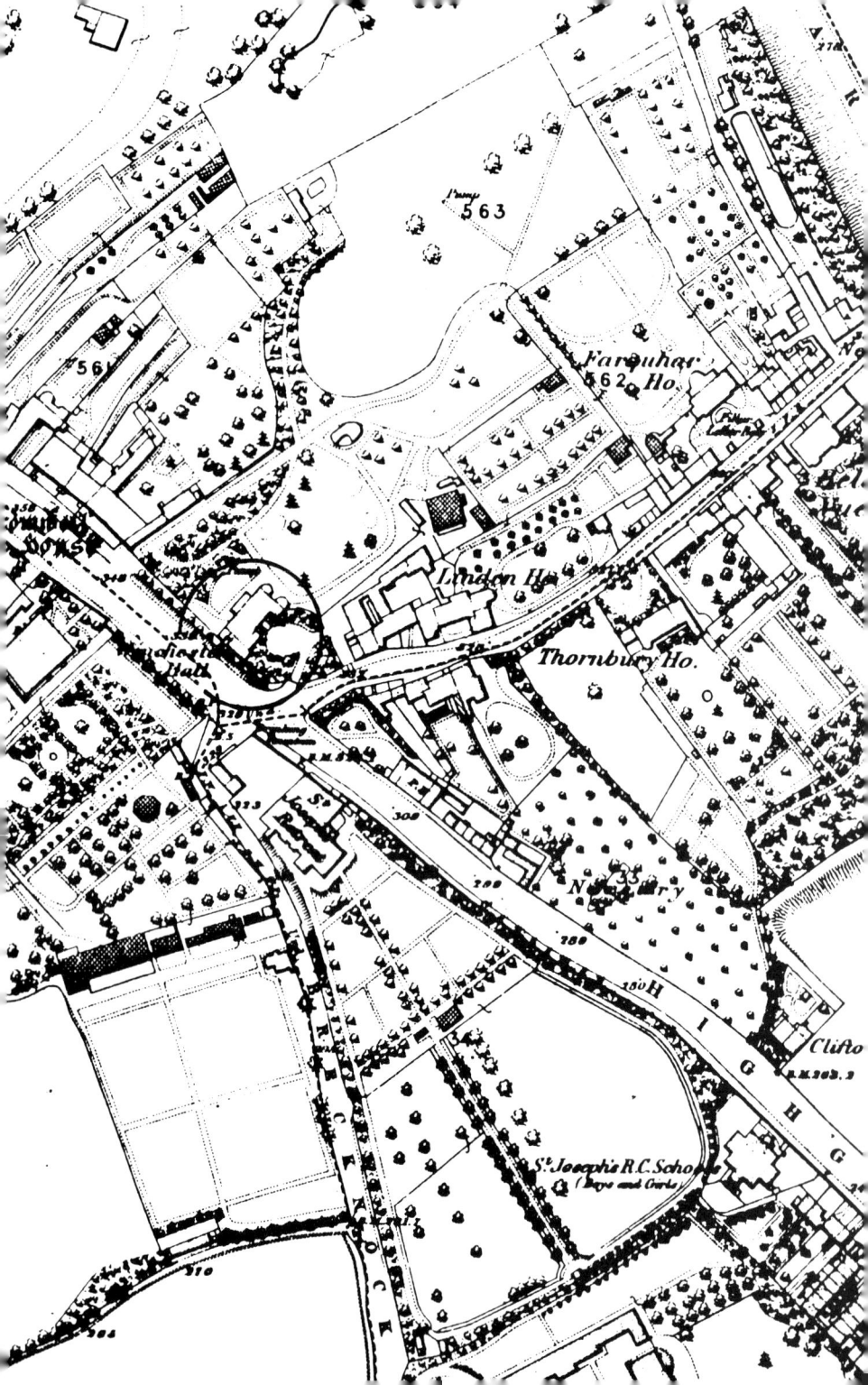

18

563

561

Farquhar
562 Ho.

Filter
Sitter Beds

Bel
H

Linden H

Thornbury Ho.

...dior
Hall

Nur...ry
33

Clifto

H
I
G
H
G

R
O
C
K

St Joseph's R.C. Scho...
(Boys and Girls)

WINCHESTER HALL, HIGHGATE
By Joan Schwitzer

By the late fifteenth century the practice of buying land in the countryside a few miles from London had become well established among City tradesmen and merchants. Suburban property was a sound investment and gave its owner the opportunity to build or acquire a spacious and impressive home for his family. Financial security and social standing were not the only benefits, however. Political power was directly related to land ownership. With a substantial acreage came the ability to elect a representative to Parliament and to have an influence in county and local affairs.

One of the districts that were particularly attractive to the potential investor was Highgate. Conveniently linked by main roads to the City, it was also considered eminently healthy. Business men were quick to realise the advantages of this growing village on the route to the north as they had those of Tottenham and Hornsey rather earlier. Some of the names of those who acquired prime sites are known from the 1460s onwards.[1] By the sixteenth century, with the increasing readiness of the chief landowner in the district, the Bishop of London, to lease parts of his wooded estate, a former hunting forest, the aristocracy were also interested. The pioneer among them was apparently Sir Roger Cholmeley, a lawyer who had been knighted under Henry VIII and had risen further to become Chief Justice of the King's Bench under Edward VI. He retired to Highgate, bought land from the Bishop, and founded the public school which was named after him but is now called simply Highgate School, that still stands at the crossroads at the summit of the High Street.

In the seventeenth century, the neighbourhood became fashionable among the gentry as a place of residence — both for those who had inherited wealth and titles, and for those who had earned them. Among them were several Lord Mayors, the first known being Sir Richard Martin. Thomas Throckmorton, the Earl of Lauderdale, Sir James Harrington, the Marquis of Dorchester, Sir Richard Sprignell, and Sir John Wollaston, were other powerful men who were the owners at various times of large houses in Highgate with splendid views. Their grounds sloped down Highgate Hill or Holloway Hill (the equivalent of the modern Highgate West Hill and Highgate Hill respectively) or looked towards Hampstead from the central green.

During the Civil Wars, Highgate was in the hands of the Parliamentarians, on whose side the City largely was. After the Restoration in 1660, its popularity with the old aristocracy, especially the Tories among them, may have declined, but Highgate was given a new attraction: it was beyond the five-mile limit of the City within which non-Anglican preachers and teachers were banned under new laws. Thus it became a refuge for Dissenters and freethinkers, including wealthy Sephardic Jews, whose numbers were remarked on by Daniel Defoe in his *Tour of Great Britain*.

One of the houses that emerge from the haze still surrounding the history of Highgate in the reign of Charles II is Winchester Hall, or possibly a predecessor on the same site. The name may have been derived in the punning fashion of the time from Susanna Winch, a widow who had once lived there. It was, at least in its later days, a redbrick building and it stood on the raised footway known as the Bank next to the junction of Highgate Hill and Hornsey Lane. It seems always to have been a large house. In 1674 it was taxed for no less than 19 hearths.[2] The owner in 1691 was Edward Beeker, a cooper and Citizen of London. By his will, dated 30th June of that year, Beeker left Winchester Hall and its grounds, as well as other property in Highgate, to his wife Elizabeth for life; after her death, it was to pass first to their daughter Elizabeth and their son-in-law John Cooke and then to their grandchildren. Two granddaughters married a London apothecary and a merchant respectively, and Mrs. Beeker was able to provide them with dowries of houses and land before she died. In 1701, her daughter, Mrs. Cooke, by then a widow, and her son, were proclaimed joint owners of Winchester Hall by the Manor Court.[3] Their successors and the fortunes of the property during the following century have not yet been discovered. (The main obstacle is the lack of an index to the chief sources — the Manor Court rolls after 1701 and the Middlesex Deeds Register).

A century later, Highgate had become a small town, but was still rural in character, being surrounded by meadows and woods. At the same time, crowded living conditions in the City were making some of those who could afford it take their families away from their business premises and move to the northern heights of London. Spacious properties like Winchester Hall, if they had been well maintained, were sure of takers. One of several contemporaries who were prominent in London commerce but brought up their families in Highgate was Peter Poland of P.R. Poland & Son, furriers in Cheapside, who also had a shop in the Strand.[4] He was living in Winchester Hall in 1812 and stayed for at least another six years.[5] He seems to have succeeded one Nathaniel Arden, or Harden, who was the Commandant of the local Volunteer force during the invasion scare about Napoleon in 1803, but it is not known exactly when he became the new occupant.[6] At some point he left Winchester Hall and moved into Farquhar House in Hornsey Lane, the Hall having been sold in about 1819. The new owner was Thomas Hurst,[7] who was a publisher from Paternoster Row, the street of "booksellers" near St. Paul's Cathedral.[8]

It was not Hurst's first house in Highgate, for since at least 1812 he had been living at a smaller residence, now known as Ivy House, higher up Highgate Hill.[9] He maintained a pied-à-terre in Bloomsbury[10] so he was obviously fairly affluent. He took an active part in local life, becoming a Governor of the Sir Roger Cholmeley Grammar School, a position he held till 1832, when he resigned.[11] Whether Hurst himself actually lived in Winchester Hall cannot at present be proved from direct evidence, since the rate books for 1818 — 1829, covering the the relevant period, have not survived. A modern writer, John Richardson, has denied it.[12] Lloyd, the author of the older *History of Highgate*, states that Hurst's brother John lived there and that Thomas lived in Farquhar House,[13] but this simply adds to the confusion. By 1829 Hurst was certainly living elsewhere, in a house of modest size, also on the Bank, and the Hall was let to one Thomas Tegg.[14] But in the meantime, in 1826, the Hursts had gone bankrupt, so that a decision to give up the Hall was to have been expected. From the record of one particular aspect of his holdings in Highgate up to the bankruptcy, it looks as if Thomas Hurst did indeed live in Winchester Hall in the 1820s. This will be explained shortly.

The Hursts's business affairs and those of their other partner, John Ogle Robinson, took several years for lawyers to sort out. They had owned property in the provinces as well as in the London area. Under the direction of the official receiver, George Lackington,[15] Hurst's estates in York were confiscated as was his London property.[16] In Highgate, friends and acquaintances seem to have made the financial penalties of extravagance much less painful. Thomas Hurst had bought Cromwell House, the large Jacobean house next door to Winchester Hall in December 1823, apparently as a speculative venture, though not entirely, as will be seen. He is known not to have been the occupier.[17] Cromwell House was taken off his hands by another School Governor, Richard Nixon.[18] Hurst had also invested in the corner site between Hornsey Lane and Highgate Hill, formerly land belonging to the Old Crown public house (which, though now re-built on that same corner, at that time lay further down the hill).[19] This plot went to Sir William Poland, son of Peter Poland. By Michaelmas 1833, Sir William was living in Winchester Hall itself.[20]

19
20

Apart from the investment value of the Cromwell House purchase, the proximity to Winchester Hall had presented an opportunity to combine the two grounds. There is evidence that Hurst seized it, and had them laid out as one entity. The map accompanying one of the post-bankruptcy agreements,[21] shows that the garden of Winchester Hall had been extended to incorporate a strip of land that had since reverted to Cromwell House. A continous sweep of lawns and paths had been created to provide pleasing walks and vistas. The motive was not simply a new and embellished path to the fields. General access to the estate was already provided for by Tile Kiln Lane further east. The landscaping could not have been done in Hurst's predecessor's time, for Peter Poland did not own the land in question. (It had belonged to William Higgins, then the owner of Cromwell House.[22]) The landscaping was clearly done by Hurst, as part of his general 'improvements' which were duly noted by the author of *The Ambulator*, published in 1820. What other motive for combining the grounds can there have been other than a wish to enjoy them during a period of residence? The back lawn with its forest trees, the sheltered kitchen garden in the angle between the grounds of Linden House and Farquhar House, the path to the shrubbery, and the flower beds and pool at the edge of the higher ground: all these elements that made up the garden in its later years were already to be seen when Sir William took over, following Hurst's departure from Highgate.

William Poland (1797 — 1884) was something of a local loyalist. He entrusted his four sons to Highgate School just after it had emerged from a law-suit which had split the ranks of the gentry, when the number of pupils had sunk to less than twenty, and when the ability of the Headmaster was being questioned and derided. The boys were all enrolled in the school between May 1833 and February 1834. Though they stayed only for preparatory schooling, its was a remarkable act of faith.[23] The four boys were Richard (born in 1821) who later went into the family fur business and lived till the age of 85,[24] Alfred (b. 1822) who became a distinguished eye surgeon at Moorfields Hospital and wrote learned medical articles, James (b. 1824) who became a naval surgeon, and Frederick (b. 1826) who graduated from Cambridge in the time-honoured way of younger sons into the clergy.[25] Little is known of their father's career beyond the fact that William Poland became Sheriff of London and Middlesex in 1831 and was knighted the same year. Sir William was a staunch Anglican, and presumably his wife too, not only supporting, as has been seen, the Grammar School Head who had also become (largely for reasons of continuity, courtesy and inertia) the Vicar of the Parish church built in 1832, but contributing towards a church school for the children of the poor that was founded in Highgate the following year.

By 1837 Winchester Hall had been acquired by Giles Redmayne,[26] a West End silk mercer. Redmayne, or 'Redmain' as it was occasionally spelled, was then about 44. He had a shop at no. 20 New Bond Street, where he sold silks and linens and lace. It had started as a family concern when he was in his early twenties,[27] and appears to have been an off-shoot of Redmayne and Lewis, Silk Mercers, of 29 Henrietta Street, Covent Garden.[28] Giles had been born in Ingleton, Yorkshire,[29] but he had probably been brought to London when he was a boy. Some Redmains were working as hosiers and haberdashers in St. John's Street, near Cloth Fair in the City, between about 1799 and 1811.[30] His opening in Bond Street suggests a man of confidence and enterprise, especially as the shop had previously been run as a completely different business (that of a "pleasure ground fence manufacturer").[31] Giles Redmayne in due course became the sole proprietor,[32] and by 1850 his son John had joined him. They branched out into additional premises nearby, at 35 Conduit Street, where they sold shawls.[33]

Giles Redmayne, though a busy man, found time for local affairs. He attended the meeetings of the Hornsey Vestry.[34] In 1839, he became the first Treasurer of the Highgate Literary & Scientific Institution founded that year.[35] He gave money towards the building of the enlarged local church schòol in 1852,[36] and was elected one of the Foundation Managers. With his business experience and broad outlook, he was successful in averting, at least temporarily, a split between the clerical and lay factions among the Managers, by the expedient of joint Secretaries.[37]

Redmayne's wife, Mary, a Londoner, had married young and had a large family which included five sons and two daughters. One, Robert, graduated from Trinity College, Cambridge,[38] and later wrote down his reminiscences of life in Winchester Hall in an unpublished manuscript which is now in the British Library. He tells us that his father, that busy family man, made no major alterations to the place during the fifteen years they lived there, but he remembered a sundial in the garden that had been made out of one of the balustrades on the old London Bridge. His brother Giles kept pigeons, and Robert himself and another brother, Mariner, had rabbits for pets. He recalled playing with the Poland children from Farquhar House and throwing stones down on to the coaches in Archway Road, from the top of the Archway that was only a few yards away from their homes. His mother used to escape to Town occasionally by taking a fly from a jobmaster's just below the Crown.[39] Keeping order in her absence were a nanny, cook, parlourmaid and housemaid,[40] a comparatively small staff for that epoch, considering the size of the house. There must also have been several gardeners. One of them lived in the grounds.

21

We do not know why this lively family left Highgate in 1852. Perhaps Mary found it too quiet after London. For a few years the Remaynes's address was near Portman Square. The business flourished, and became a limited company. In the 1860s the firm expanded into former tailoring establishments next to the New Bond Street and the Conduit Street shops. Besides selling silk fabrics, Redmayne's offered a complete dressmaking service, comprising millinery and "mantles" as well as "costumes". It continued until about 1916.[41]

The next occupant of Winchester Hall was George Sharp,[42] of whom next to nothing is known. Was he perhaps a business contact of the Redmaynes, possibly the tailor of that name in Duke Street, Mayfair?[43] Whoever he was, by the spring of 1861 the big house was empty, except for a caretaker.[44]

Later that year John William Jeakes and his family moved in.[45] Jeakes was the Director of C. Jeakes & Co., "Engineers, Stove and Range Manufacturers, Domestic Metal Workers, and General Ironmongers", of 51 Great Russell Street, near the British Museum.[46] Jeakes's forebears appear to have traded in Bloomsbury from about 1810. One John Jeakes was a carpenter and builder in Little Russell Street; coffin making led to the common accompaniment of undertaking, and he took his son into the business. Then a William Jeakes started as a general smith in the same street. From then on the family seems to have concentrated on metalworking for the builders disappear from the directories. By the mid 1820s William Jeakes was described as a 'furnishing ironmonger'.[47] His successors carried on the same trade, which greatly expanded. The Victorian era was a new iron age, of which J. W. Jeakes was one of the beneficiaries. Not only were large public buildings such as churches and railway stations constructed round an iron framework but also mutifarious domestic appliances that had previously been made in wood or earthenware were manufactured in iron.

In the 1850s Jeakes's shop gained the attention of the most popular writer of the day, Charles Dickens. It happened as follows. Florence Nightingale had written from the Crimea to her friend Angela Burdett-Coutts about the sodden misery of the British forces in the military hospital at Scutari, and advice from Dickens, who was then helping Miss Burdett-Coutts with her philanthropic work, had been sought in consequence. He advocated a drying cabinet for wet clothes and bandages, similar to that used in the Burdett-Coutts Home for women. He discovered an excellent source of supply, the "ingenious" Mr. Jeakes,[48] who indeed fulfilled his promise. He not only coped with the unprecedented requirement of shipment in parts for customer assembly but incorporated a wash-boiler and spin-drier, with a 25 minutes operating cycle, into the design. Six feet high and seven feet wide, made of iron inside a wooden cabinet, capable of drying 1,000 articles at once, Jeakes's pioneering washing machine was depicted in the *Illustrated London News* as a technical marvel. Dickens declared it was the "only solitary 'administrative' thing connected with the war that has been a *success*".[49]

After the Jeakes family moved into Winchester Hall, they fairly quickly became accepted members of the local gentry. Their wealth coupled with Jeakes's status as an officer in the local Volunteers was enough for that. But Colonel Jeakes was to gain more than mere acceptance. His enthusiastic discharge of his obligations to the less well off gained him popularity. His contributions to the life of the local community is indeed impressive. He became involved in several different voluntary efforts to supply welfare in an age without government provision. He was Treasurer of the Highgate Dispensary,[50] which was supported by private subscriptions to give free medicines to the poor. He was a J.P., which meant that he was one of six unpaid magistrates who could be called on individually to preside on a Monday at 9 a.m. at the police court. He was President of the Working Men's Club, who later paid tribute to his "grasp of mind and sound impartial judgement, tact and courtesy".[51] He strove to make the Public Health Act effective locally by bringing about a Local Board for Hornsey, and two years after it was formed in 1867 he became its Chairman.

Titled people had helped to create for Highgate, a place geographically divided between Parish authorities, a paternalistic system of administration. Since the Reform Act of 1832 and the subsequent strengthening of local as well as central government, this had come to an end. The biggest local landowner, apart from the Church, the fourth Earl Mansfield of Kenwood, was content unlike his predecessor who had died in 1840 to take a back seat in Parish affairs. People like Jeakes took his place, through what were considered the proper forms of election. But these were only open to a restricted section of the population. The ability to choose, politically as well as socially, did not extend to Society's base, the vast majority of working men, until the mid 1880s. Highgate was virtually run by a middle class obligarchy in the mid Victorian era.

The Jeakeses were also to bring vitality and colour to a neighbourhood that had become rather sedate by the 1850s. The days when the yards of some of Highgate's 23 inns had been important stopping places on the Great North Road were over. The bypass, the Archway Road, built in 1813, had taken the long distance coaching traffic, and with it a great deal of daily interest and excitement. The Jeakeses were among the first of a new wave of rich benefactors whose origins lay in trade or finance who enjoyed creating spectacular occasions for the local inhabitants and were ready to foot the bill. They were thus replacing the old aristocracy who had patronised the district, arriving and departing in splendid equipages.

In 1866 Jeakes decided to invite his old comrades in the Bloomsbury Volunteer Rifles (the 37th battalion of the Middlesex Regiment) for a field day. He had become the Highgate Commandant. On the sixth of October, a fine afternoon, 200 men assembled at three o'clock in the yard of the Foundling Hospital, and marched off under Colonel Stedall of the Highgate Volunteers. Stedall was another London ironmaster gentrified by a fine house (the Priory on Shepherds Hill) and military rank. Headed by a brass band playing, they marched up the hill and reached Winchester Hall at about four. They formed three sides of a square below the terrace. The fourth side was reserved for a large number of guests. The host made a speech of welcome, and then a display of army manoeuvres ensued. Afterwards the arms were all put in a pile, and the men were treated to a cold spread in a marquee. The officers went indoors with the other guests for refreshments. Toasts were drunk. When the force was once more on parade, there were further speeches followed by bursts of cheering. At seven o'clock the Bloomsbury Volunteers marched away.[52]

Jeakes and his wife lived in greater style than the Redmaynes, with six resident servants for themselves and their son and three daughters.[53] The entrance to Winchester Hall was suitably impressive. A belt of trees and shrubs hid the houses in the High Street. Others framed the carriage drive from the great wrought iron gates to the front steps. The property was much larger than when Hurst had bought it nearly fifty years before; the original four acres had been extended to fifteen. Jeakes owned land that had once belonged to an academy for young gentlemen, that had dwindled to a preparatory school, further along the Bank. It consisted of two meadows, one with the Cholmeley Brook running through it, and some land by the Archway Road. Jeakes decided to employ a landscape gardener to improve the estate.[54] His main contributions would seem to have been a new lower lawn, using part of the meadowland, and hothouses. Comparatively little space was devoted to an ordinary kitchen garden, but the provision of glass for raising exotic delicacies was lavish. Hothouses were increasingly a feature of the gardens of the rich. Coal to heat them was cheap, and so was labour. Gentlemen vied with each other at flower shows over their melons or pineapples. Jeakes had the great advantage of being able to order large quantities of iron at trade rates. It has been pointed out that:

> "The various forms in which cast iron became available revolutionised the hothouse. Iron bars and pulleys made it possible for panes to be opened and shut as if by a drill sergeant. Boilers came into use and cast iron pipes could release the heat where it was most needed".[55]

Two of Jeakes's greenhouses were devoted to fruit, one forty feet long for growing pineapples and a smaller one for grapes. The formal garden was terraced above the lower lawn with a hedge masking the immediate view and directing the gaze to the green slopes on the north-east where Alexandra Palace was to rise on the skyline. There were many fine trees in the grounds, poplars, limes, chestnuts, copper beeches, cedars, some of them providing interest and shade on the lawns. Other delights were the aviary, the octagonal beehive with stone steps, an ornamental pool containing water lilies, and a 'grotto' studded with shells and stones.[56]

Jeakes became President of the Highgate Horticultural Society which had been formed in the late 'fifties, and in June 1869 he lent his grounds for the annual Show. There were two large tents for the exhibits. Two police bands had been hired for the occasion and seats were provided on the lower lawn for those who wished to sit and listen. The upper lawn became a dance floor. About 3,000 people attended, and according to Jeakes not a single plant in the garden was damaged. The dancing continued until it was nearly dark. The show included the familiar fruits and vegetables arranged in classes according to whether the competitor was a 'gentleman', 'cottager' or schoolchild. Also to be seen in the marquees were peaches, pineapples, grapes, orchids, exotic ferns, and curiosities such as three-coloured geraniums (named after Highgate ladies). Novelties not entered for prizes, but intended as a contribution towards public education, included Lady Waterlow's plants raised from seed brought from Egypt, Judge Bodkin's new type of silkworms that fed on oak leaves instead of mulberry leaves, and arrangements of tropical plants from local nurseries.

The prizes were presented later, at St. Michael's School, on an evening in July. One of Jeakes's daughters carried out the task. Her father recommended other owners of large gardens to lend them as he had done. He was not in fact the first to have done so — that honour belonged to the occupants of Dufferin Lodge in 1860 — but he undoubtedly set an example of munificence and efficiency.

In 1873 Jeakes made Winchester Hall available again for the Flower Show. At the subsequent prize giving, the trophies were this time to be presented by a well known public figure who lived locally. Created a baroness two years previously for her charity work, Lady Burdett-Coutts made a speech which was partly a tribute to Jeakes.

She counselled the pursuit of advancement in life through the same "industry, energy and perseverance" which the prize winners had already displayed. She commended the Horticultural Society and Jeakes personally for being agents of social control (although she used other phrases). She expressed her particular interest in allotment gardens (for which she provided special prizes through the Society) and the recent Wild Bird Protection Act. Possibly she thought Jeakes had been instrumental in preventing breaches of it.[58]

Jeakes died suddenly on 15th February 1874, aged 57. He had not attended the meetings of the Hornsey Local Board, of which he was still Chairman, for a few weeks. He was buried in Highgate Cemetery. J. H. Lloyd, the antiquarian, had been with him on the Board and testified to the genuine regret felt.[59] He gave the Board a framed photograph of Jeakes.[60]

Jeakes's son John William inherited Winchester Hall and two-fifths of the rest of his father's estate. The remainder was divided between the girls and an annuity for their mother.[61] The family firm was eventually amalgamated with that of another iron foundry, Edward Clements. The new set-up continued in the Great Russell Street premises well into the twentieth century.[62] The Jeakes family, however, decided to move away, and Winchester Hall was sold to the Imperial Property Investment Company. Highgate was now very near the built-up areas that had spread out from Camden Town and Islington in the previous twenty years, and with the completion of the Great Northern Railway branch line from Moorgate to Edgware and the opening of Highgate Station in 1867, the district was ripe for commuter development. By April 1881 Winchester Hall was deserted, except for James Palmer, an Essex man, who was still living with his family in the gardener's cottage.[63]

The subsequent auction sales revealed the attention that had been lavished on the estate. Liberal use had been made of the Jeakes products — 1½ miles of iron fencing, wrought iron railings (some crowning the roof of the house), iron columns (perhaps those supporting the entrance hall ceiling), and the hothouse heating systems. Also for disposal were all the movable garden embellishments — the rockwork for the fernery, the beehive and aviary, and an elaborate summer house with French windows and stained glass, encased in ivy-covered imitation rock.[64] The trees were offered for timber: 100 oaks round the ancient field boundaries, and all the specimen trees in the garden; even an acacia and a yew were to be felled. There was one stipulation from the vendor in the face of the impending destruction: the grape house was not to be dismantled until after the grapes were picked.

The family had acquired a remarkable collection of paintings and furnishings. They included a portrait of Queen Elizabeth by Zucchero, another of Charles II, three portraits of a lady by Kneller, and paintings attributed to Hilliard and Lely. There were many of the trappings of a stately home — heraldic shields, pairs of antlers, a deer's head, a breastplate, and claymores and other weapons.

The furniture and pictures were sold on 18th May 1881 at Foster's Gallery in Pall Mall. The building materials were auctioned on the premises on 20th July.[65] There were no powers then to save the house nor to prevent the felling of the row of old elms on Highgate Hill outside the garden wall. The Local Board sanctioned the proposed re-development and approved the Company's plans for widening Hornsey Lane. Later they constructed a new pavement in continuation of the Bank and planted new trees.[66] One wing of Winchester Hall was taken down during July and August and the pavement diverted temporarily. To fit in with the schedule of building operations, the other wing was allowed to remain till September 1882.[67]

The house is commemorated in the names of two side roads off Cromwell Avenue (the street of terraced housing erected in its place) — Winchester Road and Winchester Place — and by the Winchester Hall Tavern in Archway Road, built at the same time.

NOTES

1. See *V.C.H.,* VI, 123
2. *Court Rolls of the Bishop of London's Manor of Hornsey 1603 — 1701,* ed. W. McBeath Marcham and Frank Marcham, 1929, p.xiv.
3. *Court Rolls,* p.226, 249.
4. Information from Gwynnedd Gosling, Librarian, H. Lit. & Sci. P. R. Poland & Son, Fur & Skin Merchants, are listed at 21 Bow Lane, Cheapside, in *Critchett's Post Office London Directory for 1836.*
5. Hornsey Rate Books; DRO 20/E2/1 and /2, G.L.R.O.
6. John Richardson, *Highgate. Its history since the fifteenth century,* Historical Publications, Barnet 1983, p.227.
7. *The Ambulator,* 1820; extract in Potter Collection of North London Topography, VII, 37: B.M. (Dept. of Prints and Drawings).
8. *London Directories:* Kent's, 1801; Holden's, 1805, 1808.
9. Hornsey Rate Book; DRO 20/E2/1, G.L.R.O.
10. Holden's *Triennial Directory,* 1817 — 1819.
11. *Highgate School Register 1833 — 1964 (Register's* 6th ed.), p.51.
12. Richardson, *Highgate,* 241
13. John H. Lloyd, *The History of Highgate......,* 1888, p.301.
14. Hornsey Rate Book, entries for April and September 1832; DRO/20/E2/4, G.L.R.O.
15. M.D.R. 1826, Book 7, No. 651.
16. M.D.R. 1832, Book 7, Nos. 650 and 651.
17. Philip Norman, *Cromwell House,* 12th Monograph of the London Survey Committee, L.C.C., 1926, p.30 — 31.
18. Norman, 31.
19. M.D.R. 1818, Book 4, Nos. 601 and 602.
20. Hornsey Rate Book; DRO 20/E2/4, G.L.R.O.
21. M.D.R. 1833, Book 3, Nos. 656 and 657.
22. Hornsey Enclosure Map, 1816; and Hornsey Rate Book 1818, DRO 20/E2/2; G.L.R.O.
23. *Highgate School Roll 1833 — 1912,* 1913 (*Register's* 1st ed.), p.40 — 41. Early enrolments, before the advent of the revered Dr. Dyne in 1838, are omitted in the 4th ed. of the *Register,* 1938.
24. Potter Coll., VI, 99.
25. Frederick Boase, *Modern English Biography,* 1897, vol. 2 (2nd. imp. 1965). cols. 1568 — 1569.
26. Hornsey Rate Book; D/PH/4C/10 (Haringey Archives), B.C.M.
27. *London Directories:* Holden's, 1822 — 4; Post Office, 1824 — 1838 eds.
28. *London Directories:* Johnstone's, 1817; Robson's, 1819.
29. Census of Hornsey, 1851, Enumerators' Returns; P.R.O. and/or B.C.M.
30. *London Directories:* Holden's, 1799, 1805 — 7 1811.
31. *London Directories:* Kelly's, 1814; Johnstone's, 1817.
32. *London Directories:* Robson's, 1826 and 1831; Pigot's, 1832 — 3 — 4.
33. Kelly's *London Directories,* 1850 and 1854.
34. Hornsey Vestry Minutes, 1838; B.C.M.
35. Info. from Librarian, H. Lit. & Sci.
36. Building Committee volume; archives of St. Michael's School, North Road, Highgate London, N.6.

NOTES *continued*

37. Managers' Minutes; archives of St. Michael's School, Highgate.
38. J. A. Venn, *Alumni Cantabrigienses....to 1900,* Part II, vol. 5. (C.U.P., 1953), p.264.
39. Quoted by Richardson, *Highgate,* 118 — 119.
40. Census of Hornsey, 1841 and 1851; P.R.O. and/or B.C.M.
41. Kelly's *London Directories,* 1853 — 1930.
42. Kelly's *Middlesex Directories,* 1855 — 1861.
43. Kelly's *London Directory,* 1844.
44. Census of Hornsey, 1861; P.R.O. and/or B.C.M.
45. Kelly's *Middlesex Directory,* 1862.
46. Kelly's *London Directories,* 1862 — 1875.
47. *London Directories:* Holden's, 1811 and 1822 — 4; Kelly's, 1814; Robson's, 1819 and 1826; Pigot's, 1826 — 7.
48. Dickens to Miss Burdett-Coutts, 21st January 1855, quoted in *Letters from Charles Dickens to Angela Burdett-Coutts 1841 — 1965,* ed. Edgar Johnson, 1953, p.284.
49. Edna Healey, *Lady Unknown,* 1978, 115 — 117. Gwynnedd Gosling (Librarian, H. Lit. & Sci.) kindly drew my attention to this passage, and identified Jeakes the heating engineer as Jeakes of Winchester Hall.
50. *Highgate Directory,* published by *The Hampstead & Highgate Express,* 1870; B.L.
51. *Highgate Parish Magazine,* vol. XII, No. 3. (March 1874), p.40; H. Lit. & Sci.
52. *Highgate Parish Mag.* vol. IV, No. 11 (Nov. 1866), p.10 — 11.
53. Census of Hornsey, 1871; P.R.O. and/or B.C.M.

54. *Highgate Parish Mag,* VII, No. 7 (July 1869), 119.
55. John Fisher, *The origins of garden plants* (Constable, 1982), p.192.
56. *O.S. 1:2500 Map, London,* 1st ed., 1870, Sheet III. See also *Catalogue* for Auction Sale on 20th July 1881 by Lerew & Oldaker, Hampstead Road; Potter Coll., VII, 39; B.M.
57. *Highgate Parish Mag.,* VII, (Aug. 1869), 138 — 141.
58. *Highgate Parish Mag.,* XI, 8 (Aug. 1873), 106.
59. Lloyd, *Highgate,* 208.
60. Hornsey Local Board Minutes, 20th April 1874, p.282; B.C.M.

61. *City Press,* 9th May 1874.
62. Kelly's *London Directories,* 1873 — 1903.
63. Census of Hornsey, 1881; P.R.O. and/or B.C.M.
64. Photograph in Potter Coll., VII, 36.
65. *Sales Catalogues,* Potter Coll., VII, 39.
66. Hornsey Local Board Minutes, 30th May 1881 (126 — 8), 8th October 1881 (388), 7th November 1881 (413 — 4); B.C.M.
67. MS note; Potter Coll., VII, 35.

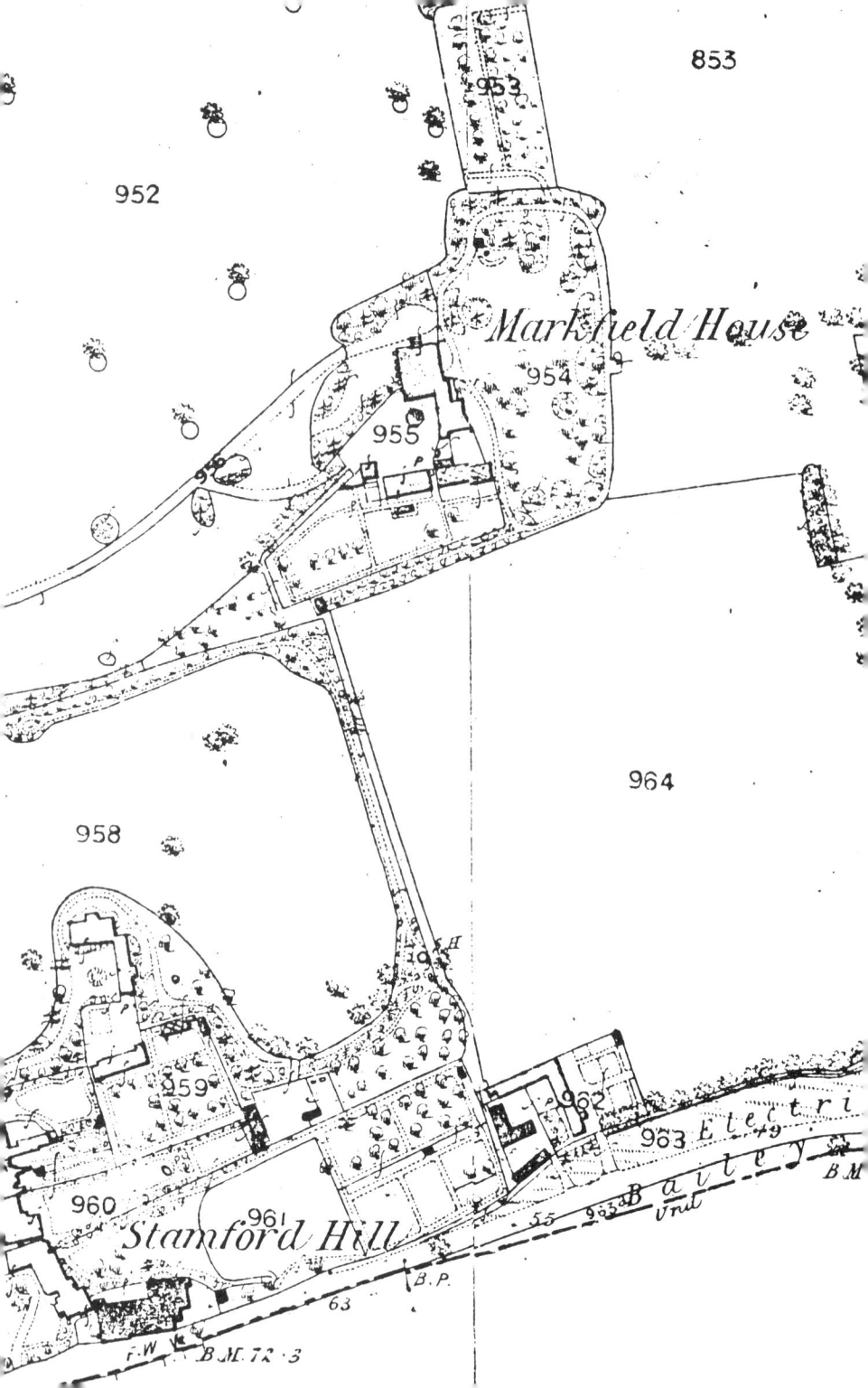

853

952

953

Markfield House

954

955

964

958

H

959

962

963 Electri

960   961

Stamford Hill   55 963 Batley

B.M

963 Vnit

B.P.

63

F.W B.M. 72·3

Markfield House

22

MARKFIELD HOUSE, TOTTENHAM
By Ian Murray

Markfield was typical of many of the larger Haringey houses in that its short lifespan reflected changing economic and social conditions in this area during the nineteenth century. It was built in 1798 when Tottenham was a fashionable rural village conveniently close to London, and stood for just 82 years when it was demolished to make way for the new streets and terraces which were turning Tottenham into a London suburb. It stood on the east side of the High Road in South Tottenham approximately between the present Lealand and Gladesmore Roads on the east side of Fairview Road. The land on which Markfield was built was low-lying and flat, drained by the Stonebridge Brook which passed through Ducketts Common and across the High Road on its way to the River Lea. Probably because of the marshy nature of the terrain this area was then still undeveloped in contrast to the higher ground to the north and south, Tottenham Green and Stamford Hill. It was on this site that William Hobson, a wealthy building contractor, chose to build a house during the 1790s.

Markfield probably existed as a distinct field in the Middle Ages, its name deriving from its proximity to the parish boundary with its markers. The earliest date, however, at which the identity and ownership of the land can be established is 1619 when according to the Field Book accompanying a survey of the Manors of Tottenham, 18 acres of pasture bearing the name Markfields had been leased by the Earl of Dorset, Lord of the Manor of Tottenham, to Edward Barkham, citizen and alderman of London, in the same year.[1] The subsequent history of the tenancy is obscure, but Markfields together with much other land in Tottenham remained part of the manor as copyhold land until some time in the 1800s when William Hobson purchased the freehold. He had in March 1793 taken out a 91 -year lease from Joseph Osgood Freame in which Hobson was somewhat surprisingly to modern ears, in view of his wealth and status, described as a Bricklayer, of Blackfields, Southwark.[2] The Tottenham poor rate books show him assessed for the land from September 1793 and assessed for the house also by April 1799.[3] It is likely that the freehold was purchased following the sale of the manors in 1805 to Sir William Curtis who enfranchised much copyhold land in order to raise capital but there appears to be no record of ths transaction in the Manor Court books. During these years, according to Robinson's *History of Tottenham,* Hobson also purchases Hillfield to the east of Markfield making a total estate of 37 acres.

William Hobson was of Quaker origins, and the father of a very large and lively family whose pleasures and relaxations were not normally associated with such a background. Very little is at present known about his early life except that he was born in November 1752 and in 1779 married Ann Richman who bore him sixteen children.[4] He was undoubtedly a very important figure in the London building and property world, becoming wealthy through land speculation, contracting, and the supply of building materials, for it was usual at that time for such men to be involved in all aspects of their business. A particularly large enterprise was the rebuilding of St. Luke's Hospital in Old Street for which Hobson in August 1782 obtained the contract for the brickwork with a tender of £9,150, the lowest of eleven. The hospital records in fact refer to Messrs. Hobson and Son, bricklayers of Horsley Down which suggests that a family business already existed.[5] The work was not completed until the end of 1788 when the total paid for the carcase of the building for which Hobson was responsible, had risen to £22,000. At the time of completion William Hobson only is mentioned, his father having probably died, and he, together with George

23

Dance the architect and Peter Banner the contractor for carpenter's work, all made a donation to the hospital and were made governors for life.[6] He is also said to have been involved in the construction of the London docks.

What led him to contemplate the move from Southwark in the 1790s to a new house in Tottenham is not known. It may have been part of a general Quaker migration into this area, a desire to be nearer his business interests, or simply to be rid of the criticisms of the Southwark Monthly Meetings. In any event, the move must have been in his mind over a long period, beginning with the initial acquisition of Markfield in 1793. The house as noted was ready in 1798 but it was apparently not until at least 1804 that the family moved in.

The acitivity with which he is particularly associated, however, did not take place until this period. This was the building of the Martello Towers, the network of military strong points along the south and east coasts for defence against a feared French invasion. Carried out by the Royal Engineers under the supervision of the Board of Ordnance, there were grave difficulties in finding a suitable contractor until Hobson was chosen in 1804. The work was sub-contracted and in 1808 his account was paid.[7] The undertaking of work on such a scale with command of the financial resources necessary indicated a man of quite exceptional power and wealth, and this Hobson undoubtedly was for his estate after his death was valued for probate at half a million pounds.[8] He was the owner of chalk pits at North Fleet, Shodland and Horking in Kent and was involved in the lime and brickmaking in association with Thomas Poynder and Son with premises at Lower Street, Islington.[9] He also held brickfields on lease near the Kingsland Road in Hackney and owned property at Dockhead, Southwark, Blackfriars, Paddington, Hackney, Scotland Yard and elsewhere.

Although nominally a Quaker, Hobson and his family found themselves so often at odds with the Southwark Monthly Meeting that his real commitment must be doubted. In 1800 it complained that Hobson "continues in the practise of paying tithes and encouraging diversions in his house". In the following year he was disowned for maintaining that he was obliged to pay tithes to comply with the law of the land.[10] Hobson's diversions were not confined to the home for he also kept a box at the opera and was addicted to hunting. (He is mentioned as hunting in Surrey by Robert Smith-Surtees, the novelist and creator of Jorrocks.) His wife was likewise criticised because "she encourages and approves of her children being taught the practise of music" and after the move to Tottenham was visited by members of the Tottenham Monthly Meeting who, because she still persisted in encouraging music and dancing at home, disowned her in October 1804. Hobson's billiard table was not approved of, nor was his sons' membership of the Volunteers for which they too were disowned. All thirteen daughters, save one who resigned herself on marriage, were eventually disowned, three for marrying out and nine for non-attendance at meetings. All the Hobson activities were unexceptional by the standards of the day for a family of their social class but were nevertheless disapproved of in Quaker circles. In later years in fact Hobson, like many former Quakers, drifted towards the established Church by whom he was buried with some pomp in 1840. He attended Tottenham vestry meetings occasionally, was a trustee of Reynardson's Almshouses and contributed to the rebuilding of the Blue School in Scotland Green in 1833 with an appropriate donation of twenty pounds worth of bricks.[11]

A pen and wash drawing of the house inserted in Robinson's own copy of his *History of Tottenham* shows a three-storied well-proportioned building in typical country house design for the period *c*.1720 — 1830. The first floor, the *piano nobile,* was of greater height than those above and in consequence had the tallest windows; the two succeeding floors were shallower with windows corresponding, the whole forming a harmonious and well-balanced rectangular facade on each face with a double pitched roof hidden behind the parapet. The construction was probably of plain brick though details of this or of the arrangement of rooms do not exist. Probably Hobson had the house built from the usual stock design, though special attention must have been paid to the requirements of the exceptionally large number of inhabitants. No photographs of the house appear to have survived.

The development of the estate itself can be traced by means of the various nineteenth century maps of the parish. In 1818[12] the house consisted of the main block with a wing adjoining on the eastern side. By 1844,[13] a further range of buildings, probably stables, coach house and other domestic offices had been added to the south and a lodge is known to have been built in 1842.[14] The arrangement remained the same in 1870.[15] The grounds included the usual lawns, kitchen gardens and orchard with wooded parkland surrounding the house, though in 1844[16] the outlying parts of the estate had been leased to James Giblett, a cattle dealer of Woodberry Lodge off St. Ann's Road. He is described as "a fox hunting looking man, never without a riding whip"[17] and obviously was well approved by the Hobsons.

The sixteen children, 13 girls and three boys were born between 1780 and 1801 and were named in order of appearance, Martha, William, Joshua, Shepherd, Anne, Susanna, Laura, Lydia, Emma, Emily, Adeline, Caroline, Hannah Blades, Georgina, Mary and Ellen. All but two of the girls married,[18] a large proportion in Tottenham Church, and one of the unmarried daughters, Hannah, is shown living at Markfield at the time of the 1841[19] Census according to the terms of her father's will which allowed such right of residence. The other occupant, apart from servants, was Adeline, who had married Captain William Babington in October 1825. One of the sons, Joshua, with his brother as trustee of his father's will, seems also to have resided at Markfield until his death at the age of 59 in 1842. According to the *Gentleman's Magazine,*[20] Joshua's demise was caused by the family addiction to the hunting field. He was thrown from his horse while fox hunting on the Devil's Dyke near Brighton, where he resided during the Season, and died soon afterwards.[21] His wife, Jane, died in the following year. William the elder son, had inherited the property on his father's death but lived in Harley Street until his own death in 1852. Of Shepherd Hobson nothing is known.

Without, however, the arrival of John Constable on a visit in 1806, the whole family might well have been abandoned to obscurity by history. Why Constable was invited to stay at Markfield is a matter of conjecture. He was thirty, unmarried, and an aspiring painter, though not certain at this stage how his art would develop. The landscapes for which he is famous were not produced until later in the decade. Certainly the prospect of the five marriageable Hobson girls would have been attractive to Constable though it is unlikely that their father would have regarded a poor and unestablished artist as a desirable nuptial proposition for any of them.

An invitation was, however sent for one reason or another and the most likely explanation is that one of Hobson's neighbours, Priscilla Wakefield, had recommended Constable as a suitable visitor to improve the girl's drawing. Priscilla Wakefield was a philanthropist and writer of children's books, and like Hobson a liberal Quaker. Though a native of Tottenham she had connections with Ipswich, and it was in the house of mutual friends, the Cobbolds, that she had first met Constable in 1799.

The sketch books[22] filled by Constable during his stay show in particular the five daughters aged between 14 and 20, Anne, Susanna, Laura, Lydia, and Emma, all highly fashionable young ladies. They also show domestic life in a large middle class country household which was contemporary with, and very similar to, the way of life portrayed in Jane Austen's novels. Emma was the most interested in reading but other activities pursued by the girls, such as drawing and embroidery, are also shown. Most interestingly, however, Constable had a fascination with hair styles which he recorded in detail. These, like the fashions, were right up-to-date and based on what were supposed to be classical styles. Plaits feature prominently, and the *Ladies Magazine* (Autumn 1806) noted that "long and regular plaits are so much the mode that, besides plaited pelerines, plaited sleeves and plaited colorettes, we have also plaited shapes". It is possible that while a guest at Markfield, Constable also made studies for his painting of All Hallows Church Tottenham which is now in Metropolitan Museum of Art, New York.

After the death of William Hobson, the house was occupied for a short time by his son, William. By 1848[23] the tenant was Michael Castilli, otherwise known as Frank, who in the 1851[24] Census is shown to be a 36 year old general merchant born in Turkey. His wife, Adele, had been born in Italy but the family had possibly lived in Edmonton before moving to Markfield as the 5 year old daughter, Mary, was born there. To look after the household which also included a son of three and Castilli's mother, there was a staff of 5 including a permanent dressmaker. Michael Castilli died a year later, and the house was successively occupied by Arthur Craven, who died in 1854,[25] and A. Drouhet. Arthur Craven apparently purchased the property on the death of William Hobson the Younger for his executors appear as owners in the ratebooks until the end.

In 1857 Charles Shaw was the occupier.[26] He is shown in the 1861[27] Census as an East India and China Merchant from Saddleworth in Yorkshire and living in the house with him were his two nieces, Mary Elizabeth Shaw and Margaret Hastings, both scholars aged 16 and 14 respectively. To attend this small household was a ladies' maid, three other servants, a gardener, under-gardener and a coachman. According to a report in the *Tottenham and Edmonton Advertiser* for June 1879 Charles Shaw had to give up possession because of the failure of a bank. The 1871[28] Census does not show him in residence but, strangely, Edward Pether, a signwriter from Islington with his wife and seven children. The ratebooks show Shaw as occupant again in 1879[29] and the house was still standing though empty in the following year. The estate was sold to developers in June 1879, and perhaps the last word should be left to the *Advertiser* which commented when reporting the sale, "like many other estates in the once rural parish of Tottenham, the land is doomed to become covered ere long with brick and mortar, and its stately mansion with its ornamental grounds will also shortly know their place no more".

NOTES

1. Acc 695/8, G.L.R.O.
2. M.D.R. 1794/95, Book 170; G.L.R.O.
3. Tottenham Poor Rate Assessment Book; D/PT/5E/1C, B.C.M.
4. Quoted in *Journal of the Friends' Historical Society,* No. 12 (1915), p.77.
5. Report of the General Committee to the Court of St. Luke's Hospital for Lunatics August 14th 1782. Court Books held at St. Luke's Woodside, Woodside Avenue, N.10.
6. C. N. French, *The Story of St. Luke's Hospital, 1750 — 1948,* Heineman, 1951, p.32. (The page in the Court book referring to this is now missing.)
7. Sheila Sutcliffe, *The Martello Towers,* David and Charles, 1972.
8. Will of William Hobson, proved July 1840; P.C.C. administrations at P.R.O.
9. S. Lewis, *The History and Topography of the Parish of St. Mary Islington,* 1842, p.51.
10. Quoted in J.F.H.S. as above.
11. William Robinson, *The History and Antiquities of the Parish of Tottenham,* 2nd ed. 1840, p.264, 305.
12. Survey of the Parish of Tottenham made in 1818;B.C.M.
13. Tithe Map, Parish of Tottenham 1844; D/PT/3A/4, B.C.M.
14. Poor Rate Assessment Book, Parish of Tottenham, 1842; B.C.M.
15. *25" Ordnance Survey of the Parish of Tottenham,* 1870; B.C.M.
16. Tottenham Rent Charge Book, 1843; D/PT/3A/3, B.C.M.
17. Unpublished account of St. Ann's Road in the 1860s; typescript, B.C.M.
18. *Middlesex Parish Registers (Marriages) Vol. IX (Tottenham),* Phillimore, 1938.
19. Enumerator's returns, Parish of Tottenham, 1841 census; microfilm copy, B.C.M.
20 *Gentleman's Magazine* cutting and additional information contained in William Robinson's *History,* vol. 1, p.123, as above.
21. *Ibid.*
22. Published in *Constable and his friends in 1806,* ed. G. Reynolds, Trianon Press, 1981.
23. Poor Rate Assessment Book, Parish of Tottenham 1848; B.C.M.
24. Enumerator's returns, Parish of Tottenham, 1851 census; microfilm copy, B.C.M.
25. Poor Rate Assessment Book, Parish of Tottenham, 1854; B.C.M.
26. Poor Rate Assessment Book, Parish of Tottenham, 1857; B.C.M.
27. Enumerator's returns, Parish of Tottenham, 1861 census; microfilm copy, B.C.M.
28. Enumerator's returns, Parish of Tottenham, 1871 census; microfilm copy, B.C.M.
29. Poor Rate Assessment Book, Parish of Tottenham, 1879; B.C.M.

120

119

121

Brook House

122

118

123

126

117

Brunswick Nursery

Brunswick Brewery

115

116

125

B. Chapel

Chapel Place

38

Globe House

B.M. 43

The Vicarage

The Yews

41

231

232

234

CHARLES STREET

WILLIAM STREET

37

30

41

STREET

Brook House

BROOK HOUSE
By Jean Pegram

Unlike so many of our "lost houses", Brook House existed within living memory. It was a very private house quite lacking in the ostentatious prominence of its more palatial contemporaries. Throughout its long life this house seems to have been a home rather than a landmark, and tending for this reason to be rather less well known than it deserved to be. As a visitor to the house in 1956 recalled: "The only signs of the existence of Brook House from the High Road at Snells Park boundary when I was a child, was a great white painted wooden carriage gate set between pillars in a high brick wall screened at both front and rear by lime trees on a verge of green grass which has long since disappeared. Today only trees and wall remain and a gap where the gate once stood reveals a monstrous factory".[1]

The virtual "invisibility" of Brook House may have been the factor which caused it to be overlooked by Tottenham's foremost historian, William Robinson, and also the more recent Fisk and Roe. Robinson wrote extensively about the larger estates and even the quite trivial recently built villas of his time but mentioned Brook House only in passing. In a scarcely recognisable reference, identifying the property only by location, and the names of contemporary occupants, he suggested a connection between the house and a long lost Manor of Tottenham, mentioned by William Bedwell in 1631.[2]

At the close of the last century the Brook House Estate somewhat curiously failed to attract the interest of the developers. It came on to the market in the year 1897, but was bought in at an auction for the sum of £2,000.[3] The site occupied some 3 acres on the north-western corner of Tottenham High Road's boundary with Edmonton and contained an early seventeenth century mansion with out-buildings. Why it was not sold remains a mystery, but this accident of fate, if such it was, ensured a further fifty-nine years of useful life for a house of quite remarkable charm and character, and certainly the oldest domestic building still in private occupation in the Tottenham area.

Brook House was included in the Royal Commission's Survey of Historic Monuments in 1937. The report dated the building as early 17th century, but concluded that it was remodelled and refaced about 1700. The house consisted of two storeys with attics. On the east front the two wings retained their eaves cornices of c.1700, but the space between had been filled in by a modern addition. Behind this was a doorway of c.1700, flanked by fluted corinthian columns supporting an entablature with the architrave turned up in the middle and cherub-heads over the columns. The inside of the building contained some early 17th century moulded ceiling beams and some doors and door frames of the same date. There was also early 18th century and Georgian panelling and an early 18th century fireplace with marble surround. An extensive photographic survey of the house was taken by the County Planning Officer in 1955. One of the features depicted was a beautifully carved oak staircase, remarkably similar in design to the west wing staircase at Bruce Castle; both perhaps the work of a local craftsman.

Brook House was probably not known as such until early in the 19th century.[4] The name does not appear to be associated with either the Moselle to the south or Pymmes Brook to the north, but possibly with an underground tributary from either which gave rise to a large stretch of ornamental water in the grounds; a further stretch of water backed the houses in Brook Place a little to the south of Brook House.[5] Two of the houses in Brook Place, built in about 1710, still exist, and have recently been restored.[6]

25

26

The earliest traceable owners of the house were the Mallorys and it formed part of Andrew Mallory's widow's estate in the year 1619.[7] The house at this time was described as "a cotage or tenement with a Barne Orchard and backside to ye same belonging now in the tenure of Thomas Yunian", (or Ynnian). The grounds occupied just over 3 acres; together with the adjoining 13 acres of pasture, another 3 acres of pasture in High Cross Lane and 5 acres of arable land in the Hale it constituted a fair-sized estate of which Thomas Yunian was the tenant farmer. From earliest times, Tottenham's farmers had been the tenants of land-hungry city merchants, who amassed for themselves considerable estates on the outskirts of London. This land provided them with revenue, political power and country retreats close to the Metropolis; of just such a kind were the Mallorys of Tottenham.

Sir Richard Mallory was a member of the Mercer's Company and Lord Mayor of London, 1564 — 65. According to Stowe:

> "He dwelt in Cheapside at the sign of the Golden Key.........the messuage wherein he dwelt having been some religious possession came into the hands of Edward VIth who in his second year sold it to the said Mallory for £128 — with all other houses, edifices, shops, cellars, terraces, stables and gardens, thereunto belonging of the yearly value of £8. Thus much for the High Street of Cheap".[8]

Mallory's Tottenham property was also very extensive and included his country house, though it is difficult to identify its exact whereabouts today.[9] He died in the year 1566 and was buried in the Mercers' Company's Chapel in Leadenhall Street. According to the custom of Tottenham Manor his copyhold lands in Tottenham were inherited by his youngest son, Edward, who was then only ten years of age.[10] Little is known of the young Edward's life, but a substantial part of it must have been spent in Tottenham, for he was buried in the old Parish Church of All Hallows in the year 1603. It is significant that in this year the Parish Clerk recorded no fewer than 43 deaths from the "Peste", out of a total of 70 burials. Few survived middle age in these times and plague was a recurring factor in the high mortality rate. One wonders to what a degree London's rich citizens, escaping the pestilence in the City, were responsible for transmitting the infection to their country estates. Infant mortality was correspondingly very high, even amongst the wealthiest of families, and it would seem that in this the Mallorys were no exception. Edward Mallory appears to have died without heirs, as did his older brother Andrew; a third brother Richard left a son William, who in turn died without heirs in the year 1615.[11] After the death of Elizabeth, widow of Andrew Mallory, the Brook House Estate was claimed by Robert Barkham, and the next chapter in its history follows along remarkably similar lines.[12]

The Barkhams may be seen as the Stuart counterparts of the Tudor Mallorys. Robert Barkham was the younger son of another prominent Tottenham landowner, Sir Edward Barkham, who was a member of the Drapers' Company and Lord Mayor of London, 1621 — 22.[13] In the year 1625 Robert Barkham married Maria, the 17 year old daughter of Richard Willcocks of Tottenham.[14] Maria bore him twelve children and died in 1644 at the age of 36. The sculptured effigies of Robert and Maria Barkham and ten of their children in Jacobean dress constitutes one of the most beautiful of the surviving monuments in All Hallows Church. We do not know for certain if Robert and Maria Barkham lived in Brook House, but the former "cotage" would seem to have been substantially re-built at about the time of their marriage.

There is no doubt, however, that after the death of his father in the year 1636, Robert demised, or let, the house and estate to his mother, Dame Jane Barkham, possibly in exchange for the late Sir Edward's mansion at High Cross. At this point

Brook House seemingly became the Barkham "dower house" until the death of Dame Jane in the year 1660. Robert Barkham received a knighthood from Charles I in 1641, by which time he had also acquired a considerable estate in Lincolnshire. Thus the family, with its origins in successful trade, entered the higher ranks of the landed genty. Sir Robert Barkham died in 1661 and his property in Tottenham and Edmonton was left in trust for his 17 year old son, Robert.[15]

Later in the 17th century the property was acquired by the Ambrose family, who held it for several generations. The original estate had by now been enlarged to include Brook Place to the south and the sites of Clay Hill Lodge and River House to the west. This now extensive estate remained intact until the middle years of the 19th century.[16] In the year 1711 Sir Thomas Ambrose died and the property passed to his widow, Dame Anna. The record refers to it as "formerly the perquisite of Sir Robert Barkham", and "formerly in the occupation of Thomas Boulton and John Russell"; presumably the tenant farmers. It goes on: "Upon which the premises, (three) newly erected and built".[17] The year 1711 would then seem to have been the date of the substantial alteration of Brook House and the building date of two houses in the adjoining Brook Place. On the death of Dame Anna in the year 1719, her son, the second Sir Thomas Ambrose claimed the estate. By now Brook House and Brook Place were in the occupation of Thomas Ambrose, Daniel Bell[18] and John Chancellor respectively.

The second Sir Thomas Ambrose was described as "Knight, Citizen and Brewer of London". Although he died in Tottenham he was, according to the Parish Register, "carried to Aldgate to be buried, February 27th, 1725/26 — Lady Ambrose carried away December, 22nd, 1728". Whereas Sir Thomas Ambrose or his son, also Sir Thomas, appear to have lived in the enlarged Brook House of c.1710, by the year 1720 the three houses on the estate were occupied by Thomas Morris, John Morris and William Morris. Abraham Ambrose, the younger son of Sir Thomas, succeeded to the estate in 1729, following which it changed hands completely in the year 1735.[19] In the *Gentleman's Magazine* of 1732 there is a revealing reference to the marriage of: "Sir Thomas Ambrose, Brewer in Houndsditch, to a niece of the late dowager Countess of Coleraine (of Bruce Castle) with a £20,000 fortune". Marriages in the eighteenth century were largely contracted as a means of social and economic advancement.

After Thomas Ambrose, Brook House never seems to have been occupied by its owner, but by a series of often equally affluent tenants on a twenty-one year lease agreement. We know that Thomas Morris lived there in the year 1720, but throughout the succeeding seventy or so years all references to the house in the records describe it only as "formerly in the occupation of Thomas Morris." The Morris family were yeoman farmers. For many generations they were customary tenants of the Manor for farmland in Wood Green. Their names appear over and over again in the records throughout the 16th, 17th and 18th centuries. One Thomas Morris was a churchwarden in 1686 and, another, possibly his grandson, was steward of the Manor of Tottenham in 1762. This was a family that had its roots in Tottenham. The merchant adventurers came and went, but the Morrises farmed the land and by the very substance of their presence were the natural leaders of the local community.

This now considerable estate was acquired in 1735 by Thomas Grace, about whom little is known. He seems to have had no immediate family for the lands passed to his brother Nicholas after his death in 1742. Nicholas Grace also left no wife or children and the Tottenham property was inherited on his death, in 1743, by a niece, Elizabeth Massa. Elizabeth, the daughter of Thomas Massa of Mansell Street in Whitechapel, was a spinster at the time she claimed her inheritance, and a spinster she remained for the ensuing twenty-one years. This in itself was unusual for a woman of means in the 18th century. Elizabeth's name gives cause for further specualtion. The name Massa is rare and may have origins of unusual interest.[20] Elizabeth married in 1764, the year before her death.[21] Her husband was Charles Hornby of the Pipe Office[22] and of Ormand Street in Holborn. Elizabeth died without children and her husband was the sole beneficiary under her will.[23]

Elizabeth Massa kept her Tottenham property in good order. Unlike so many of Tottenham's absentee landlords she was never summoned before the Manorial Court for neglect of her premises: indeed, in 1762 she obtained the required licence from the Lord of the Manor to fell trees "for the necessary repair of her houses barns stables erections and fences".

In about 1754 Elizabeth Massa leased Brook House to Dr. Matthew Clarke.[24] This distinguised physician seems to have retreated to Tottenham in his early fifties, having retired somewhat prematurely from an outstanding medical career. He was born in London in 1701 and at the age of twenty "entered the physic line at Leyden", Leyden University in Holland being the foremost seat of medical learning in its time. After he was created Doctor of Medicine at Cambridge in 1728, Dr. Clarke commenced a long career at Guy's Hospital, to which he was elected Physician in March 1732, a post which he held for the next twenty years. In 1736 he was elected a Fellow of the (Royal) College of Physicians and was Censor of the College in 1743.[25] It is some indication of the esteem in which he was held that on his resignation from Guy's in January 1754, he was elected a Governor of the Hospital. The only evidence of his contribution to the medical knowledge of his day is his Latin 'Dissertation on Pleurisy' which he read at Leyden in 1726; a copy of this is held in the British Library. Of his contribution to life in Tottenham over a period of twenty or so years there is also very little recorded, but through the terms of his will he did convey something of his concern for the elderly poor of the Parish. He left £600 in trust, the dividends from which were to be paid throughout her life to a Mrs. Pearce, widow of a former colleague and surgeon at Guy's Hospital; on her death the sum was to be invested in stock or security, and the dividends paid annually to the residents of Reynardson's Almshouses in Tottenham.[26] The money was to be shared equally among the inhabitants at Christmas. This bequest was augmented some years later by another inhabitant of Brook House, which would seem to have generated charitable impulses in its occupants.

Dr. Clarke's next door neighbour, in Brook Place in 1777, was Mr. Rivers Dickinson.[27] After the death of Matthew Clarke in 1778, Rivers Dickinson and family moved into Brook House. The Dickinsons were a long -established Tottenham family, and it may have been the influence of his neighbour which caused Matthew Clarke to endow the Reynardson Almshouses, for Rivers Dickinson was elected a trustee of this institution in 1777.[28] His father, also Rivers Dickinson, had been one of the first trustees appointed in the year 1734.[29] The Dickinsons were brewers in St. John's Street, Clerkenwell[30] and seem to have had earlier connections with Ware in Hertfordshire, for it was here in 1742 that a sermon was preached on the occasion of the death of the first Rivers Dickinson of Tottenham. The sermon delivered by one Ebenezer Fletcher, a member of the family, was published in the following year. The oration refers to the deceased's "great humanity and tender compassion for widows and orphans in their affliction", his honesty and integrity, and, "notwithstanding the temptations that persons of his business are particularly exposed to, so far as I could observe as strict temperance as I knew".[31]

27

28

Rivers Dickinson of Brook House was imbued with many of his father's virtues; he was also an extremely able business man for in addition to the family brewery, responsibility for which he shared first with his brother Samuel and then his sons, he seems to have had connections with the East India Company. This family connection with the East India Company was sustained, for his grandson, John Docwra Dickinson, was Secretary to the Court of Directors of the Company in the year 1830.[32] Rivers Dickinson was buried in the East India Company's Chapel in Poplar in 1786, where he was later joined by his wife, Sarah.[33]

In 1781, the ownership of the Brook House Estate passed, on the death of Charles Hornby, to his brother William.[34] William Hornby, or Captain Hornby, as he is referred to in earlier records, lived during the latter part of his life in Brook Place, with his young wife Martha, who outlived him by thirty-five years. Little is known of his career, but he too may have had connections with the East India Company. His near neighbour in Brook Place was Mary Metcalf, widowed daughter of Rivers Dickinson, whilst in Brook House itself lived her mother Sarah Dickinson.

The widowed Sarah Dickinson lived on in Brook House until her death in 1802. She was undoubtedly a lady of "good works" but her charity was not without its bounds. One of the local charities to benefit from her will was the recently established Green School or School of Industry for Girls, an institution founded by that distinguised local quaker and philanthropist, Priscilla Wakefield, in 1792. Priscilla Wakefield recorded in her diary in October 1798: "Spent the day at Mrs. Dickinson's. My indignation rose at the uncharitable remarks of a fine lady at the hospitality shown to the French emigrants".[35] (These emigrants were refugees from Napoleonic France and the founders of the St. Francis de Sales Catholic Church in Tottenham). The Green School benefitted from Sarah Dickinson's will, to the order of £20, and she also left £20 to the Blue Girls' Charity School at Scotland Green and £200 worth of consol shares to that favourite institution of the family, Reynardson's Almshouses.[36]

Sarah Dickinson was followed at Brook House by her second daughter, the widowed Sarah Beachcroft. She upheld family tradition by endowing Reynardson's Almshouses; she also made a further bequest, to the group of almshouses established by Balthazar Sanches, in her will which was proved in 1834.[37] Sarah Beachcroft left her Tottenham home to spend her remaining years in Blunham in the county of Bedford. She was succeeded in the tenancy of Brook House by the exotically named Cajaton Dias Santos, somewhere about the year 1818.[38]

In 1815 Dias Santos & Co. were merchants trading from No. 18 Great Winchester Street, and a few years later from No. 39 Bucklersbury, Cheapside.[39] In what kind of merchandise they traded, the age and origin of the firm, and what position Cajaton Dias Santos held within it, is unknown. This family was in all probability Portuguese, but established in this country over some length of time. (A Miss Anne Dias Santos was buried in Pancras Churchyard in 1788, a churchyard noted as the burial place for Catholics living in London and its environs in the 18th century.)[40] We do not know what in particular drew Dias Santos to Tottenham, though he may have had trading connections with families in the area. It is also significant that a small Catholic chapel had been erected in Queen Street in 1805, and that Tottenham was noted for its tolerance to strangers. However, Dias Santos seems also to have involved himself with the affairs of the old Parish Church of All Hallows. In the year 1819 the silver communion plate was stolen from the church and he was one of the six local inhabitants to donate silver in replacement of that which was stolen.[41] His name was also amongst those who attended the funeral procession of the much respected vicar, the Rev. Thomas Roberts, in October 1824.

This most impressive affair, described in detail by William Robinson, seems to have included all the local notability. Cajaton Dias Santos, Esq., was on the list of "Private Carriages with Company".[42]

In the early years of the century the owner of the estate, Martha Hornby, vacated her house in Brook Place, re-married, and as Martha Budgeon, moved to a larger house on the opposite side of the High Road, where she lived until her death in 1836. Her house in Brook Place was taken over by Nathaniel Stonard who, in turn, moved into Brook House itself after Dias Santos left in 1828.[43] He occupied it only briefly, for he died in 1833. Nathaniel Stonard seems to have been a gentleman farmer, originally of Bromley in Kent, who left a fair fortune of £16,000 to his widow Susannah. Susannah Stonard lived on in Brook House for a further seventeen years, and when she died in 1850 her estate was valued at £12,000.[44] After this long spell of occupation by a childless widow Brook House became a family home once more in 1851.

In the meanwhile, the ownership of the estate had passed on the death of William Hornby's widow in 1836 to his second cousin, Barnard Baker, a farmer of High Ongar in Essex.[45] No doubt Barnard Baker continued to farm his land in Essex for the remainder of his working life but settled on his retirement in Brook Place, like his cousin before him, with his wife Harriet, and a son and daughter. It was here that he died in 1892 aged 83; his son, Alfred Barnard Bacon Baker, the last known owner of the estate, was admitted as a customary tenant of the Manor in the same year.[46]

In 1860 the *Tottenham and Edmonton Advertiser* carried an advertisement for "Frith's Celebrated Quinine Wine", which could be purchased at Mr. Wall's, the Chemist's, in the High Road, for two and sixpence per bottle. The advertisment concluded: "Caution — None are genuine unless capsuled with the name and address — 'J. Frith's Quinine Wine, Bishopsgate Street, London''. James Frith and his family occupied Brook House for about eight years from 1851, when his household consisted of his wife, six children, cook, housemaid and gardener. Strangely enough the house which had earlier been associated with brewers, then a tonic wine manufacturer, was next occupied by a Ginger Beer and Mineral Water Manufacturer, who perhaps even more strangely, was also a woman. Mrs. Rawlings, presumably a widow, remarried in about 1861 and caused confusion for the Census Enumerator of that year, as his entry describes her as Sarah Doo Rawlings — with the "Rawlings" deleted — aged 42, the wife of Henry Doo, aged 26, also a Mineral Water Manufacturer, and two sons, Henry Rawlings, aged 15, a sailor, and Arthur Rawlings, aged 7.

The two remaining tenants of Brook House about whom information is available from the Census records were, first, James Girling, a coal merchant, who was living there in 1871 with his wife, Elizabeth, and four daughters, and second, Alfred Nelson, a manufacturer, with his wife Ann, two sons and a daughter, who were living there in the year 1881. From the year 1898 and for the remainder of its life Brook House was occupied by just one family, the Klemantaskis.

The north-western corner of Tottenham High Road in the 1890s displayed a rather uneasy combination of residential and industrial elements. The former gardens backing Brook Place had been sold off to Pickfords the road haulage firm by 1893, and small industrial workshops and warehouses occupied much of the land between the High Road and the Great Eastern Railway line to the south of Brook House. It was a compromise between these factors that the new occupier, Maurice Klemantaski, brought to Brook House in the year 1898. He kept the house as a family home and the gardens as a domestic amentity, but consigned the northern perimeter of the estate to industrial use in the form of a small family factory known

29

30

31

as the Boundary Wool and Hair Mills. Details concerning the firm's output and distribution are not available but the factory seems to have employed only a small local workforce and yet remained a viable enterprise for at least the succeeding 50 years. With the advent of modern synthetic materials and changing fashions in the furniture industry, the market for hair declined and in the post-war years the firm specialised under the name of Associated Wool Mills; it was listed in the year 1955.

Maurice Louis Klemantaski was Dutch by previous nationality, though his name implies Polish origins. In December 1891, he married Deborah Jaffa at the New Synagogue in Fenchurch Street.[47] At the time of her marriage Deborah was living in Dalston, but she had been born in the small town of Fitzroy, near Melbourne, in Australia.[48] Her father was Solomon Jaffa and his name suggests an interesting lineage.[49]

The Klemantaskis had three children, two sons and a daughter. The elder son, Harry Maurice Jaffa Klemantaski was educated at the Latymer Grammar School in Edmonton; he later became a prominent member of the tennis section of Edmonton Cricket Club, and took part in many open tournaments. With his father and younger brother, Louis Philip Jaffa, he was one of the principals of the Associated Wool Mills until his early tragic death at the age of 50. He was killed in a road accident in February 1943, during wartime black-out conditions. Maurice Klemantaski remained actively associated with the firm until his death in January 1946, when he was in his 80th year. His younger son Louis, a life-long bachelor, was still with the firm when it closed. The daughter of the family, Alida Evelyn, married but is not known to have borne children.

Deborah Klemantaski, who died in January 1941, was a much loved and respected public figure. Most of her life's energy and interest was devoted to charitable work, with particular regard to the welfare of children. She worked for both national and local major institutions. She was President of the Invalid Children's Aid Association and President of the Tottenham Branch of the N.S.P.C.C. She was also very active in the W.V.S. and the Ladies' Association of the Prince of Wales's Hospital in Tottenham. It was her great love of children and seemingly inexhaustible drive in working for the benefit of others that impressed people most.

Brook House was demolished in 1956. Had it survived for just a few more years then much of its former beauty might well have been restored and its future assured. It is unlikely that a house of such interest and quality would be destroyed in such a regardless fashion today.

NOTES

1. Lily Hawkes, "Houses of Tottenham", typescript, 1957;B.C.M.
2. William Robinson, *History and Antiquities of the Parish of Tottenham*. 2nd. ed., 1840, vol. I, p.254.
3. *Plan and Particulars of Sale, May, 1897, "Freehold Estate known as Brook House",* Tottenham Sales of Property with Plans, vol. II; B.C.M.
4. The house cannot be identified by name before this period, but it is interesting to note that a "messuage' (house with outbuildings and land), described as "Brokkys", was held by Thomas Stubbs in 1511; as "Brokes", held by Edward Banks in May 1559, and as "Brookes", held by Sir Richard Mallory in December, 1559. Tottenham Borough Council, *Manor of Tottenham: Published translations of the Court Rolls,* vols. 6 and 9; B.C.M.
5. Survey Map of Tottenham Parish, 1818; B.C.M.
6. Now numbered 867 and 869 High Road.
7. Manor of Tottenham: Field Book to the Parchment Plan taken in 1619; Acc. 695/9, G.L.R.O. (B.C.M. Micro.)
8. Stowe's *Survey of London,* 1754 edition.
9. *Manor of Tottenham: Published translations of the Court Rolls,* vol. IX; B.C.M.
10. *Court Rolls,* vol. VIII; B.C.M.
11. Manor of Tottenham: Court Roll, 1615. Unpublished translation; B.C.M.
12. In the year 1619 Robert Barkham claimed a "reversionary interest" in the estate, which was held in four parts.
13. Stowe's *Survey of London.*
14. *Middlesex Parish Registers, Tottenham Marriages Abstracts, vol. IX,* Phillimore Press, 1938; B.C.M.
15. Manor of Tottenham: Court Baron, 1661; unpublished translation, p.23—24, B.C.M.
16. Parish of Tottenham: Rent Charge Book, 1843, p.13—15; PT/102A/3, B.C.M.
17. Manor of Tottenham Court Rolls, 1626 — 1792 (Copy); Acc. 695/1, G.L.R.O. (B.C.M. Micro.)
18. Daniel Bell was the grandfather of Priscilla Wakefield. See note 35.
19. Manor of Tottenham Court Rolls, 1733 — 35; Acc. 695/5, G.L.R.O. (B.C.M. Micro.)
20. Massa is an Italian city, and also a Moroccan port; its occurrence as a surname in this country is rare. Fortuna ("formerly Cooba") Massa was registered as an occupant of the House of Converts, 1580 — 1601. *Middlesex and Herts. Notes and Queries,* vol. II, 1896.
21. *Gentleman's Magazine,* 1754.
22. The Pipe Office contained the Pipe Rolls which were the accounts rendered by the Sheriffs to the Exchequer.
23. Will of Elizabeth Hornby, 1765. See Tottenham Manor Court Baron, 18th October 1765; Admission of Charles Hornby; Acc. 695/5, G.L.R.O. (B.C.M. Micro.)
24. Tottenham Parish Poor Rate Books. File commences 1777; B.C.M.
25. W. Munk, "Roll of the Royal College of Physicians", p.131; Wellcome Institute for the History of Medicine. See also *Dictionary of National Biography.*

NOTES *continued*

26. Will of Matthew Clarke (Dr./Physic), P.C.C., Proved 1.12.1778; P.R.O.
27. Tottenham Parish Poor Rate Books; B.C.M.
28. Reynardson's Almshouses: Minute Books of the Trustees; D/PT/7C, B.C.M.
29. Robinson, *Tottenham,* vol. II, p.261.
30. Baldwin's *London Directory,* 1770 & 1775; G.L. Kent's *London Directory,* 1783; G.L. Critchett and Woods *P.O. Directory,* 1815 & 1818; Postal History Collection, B.C.M.
31. *A Funeral Sermon preached at Ware in Hertfordshire, Dec. 29th 1742. On the occasion of the death of Mr. Rivers Dickinson of Tottenham in Middlesex,* By Ebenezer Fletcher, Printed for R. Hett at the Bible and Crown in The Poultry, 1743; B.C.M.
32. *Bengal Past and Present,* vol. 27, p.204; India Office Library.
33. Lysons' *Environs of London,* vol. V, 1811, p.295.
34. Manor of Tottenham Court Rolls: Court Baron, 13.2.1781. Admission of William Hornby; Acc. 695/6, G.L.R.O. (B.C.M. Micro.)
35. Extracts from the Diaries of Priscilla Wakefield are contained in the Hazel Mews' Collection at the Library of the Religious Society of Friends, Friends' House, Euston Road.
36. Dickinson, Sarah, P.C.C. Will, proved 3.11.1802; P.R.O.
37. Beachcroft, Sarah, P.C.C. Will, proved 1834; P.R.O.
38. In November 1816, Cajaton Dias Santos, of Lansdown Place, Hackney, took the lease of Clay Hill Lodge (Devonshire Hill Lane), on the Brook House, Estate. Court Rolls; Acc. 695/7, G.L.R.O. (B.C.M. Micro.)

39. Santos, Manoel Dias & Co., Abchurch Lane, Lombard Street; Baldwin's *London Directory,* 1770; G.L. Dias Santos & Co., Merchts., 28 Gt. Winchester Street; Critchet & Woods *P.O. Directory,* 1815 and 1818; Postal History Collection, B.C.M.
40. Lysons', *Environs of London,* vol. III, p.358.
41. and
42. Robinson, *Tottenham*
43. Tottenham Parish Poor Rate Books; B.C.M.
44. Stonard, Nathaniel, P.C.C. Will, 1833; P.R.O. Stonard, Susanna, P.C.C. Will, 1850; P.R.O.
45. Tottenham Manor: Special Court Baron, 22.11.1836, admission of Barnard Baker on the death of Martha Budgeon; Acc. 695/8, G.L.R.O. (B.C.M. Micro.)
46. Tottenham Manor, 1892; Acc. 695/4, G.L.R.O. (B.C.M. Micro.)
47. In the year 1913 this synagogue was removed from the City and re-erected brick by brick in Egerton Road, Stamford Hill.
48. Register of Jewish Marriages, Office of the Chief Rabbi, Alder House, Tavistock Square, W.C.1.
49. For information relating to the descendants of Rabbi Mordecai Jaffe, see *A Light unto my path. The story of H. N. Solomon of Edmonton,* by Jeffrey & Barbara Baum, E.H.H.S. Occasional Paper, No. 43.

INDEX OF PERSONS AND PLACES
Numbers in bold type indicate illustrations